P9-BZD-262

# Kabbalah, Science and the Meaning of Life

Rav Michael Laitman, PhD

# Kabbalah, Science and the Meaning of Life

LAITMAN
KABBALAH PUBLISHERS

Rav Michael Laitman, PhD

Translation: Chaim Ratz
Proofreading: Kate Weibel
Editor: Claire Gerus
Drawings: Avi Ventura
Layout: Baruch Khovov
Cover Design: Richard Aquan
Printing and Post Porduction: Uri Laitman

---

Laitman Kabbalah Publishers Website:
**www.kabbalah.info**
Laitman Kabbalah Publishers E-mail:
**info@kabbalah.info**

---

KABBALAH, SCIENCE
AND THE MEANING OF LIFE

---

ISBN: 0-9738268-9-4
FIRST EDITION: OCTOBER 2006

# Kabbalah, Science and the Meaning of Life

## TABLE OF CONTENTS

# FOREWORD

The essence of human nature is its perpetually evolving desire for pleasure. To realize this desire, we feel compelled to discover, invent, and improve our reality. The gradual intensification of the desire for pleasure has been the force behind human evolution throughout our history.

The desire for pleasure evolves through several stages. In the first stage, it manifests in the need for sustenance, such as food, reproduction, and family. In the second stage, the desire for wealth arises, and in the third, there is a craving for honor, power, and fame. Development of these three stages had lead to major changes in human society—it became a diversified, multi-class society.

The fourth stage signifies our yearning for learning, knowledge and wisdom. This expresses itself in the development of science, educational systems, and culture. This stage has become associated with the Renaissance and the Scientific Revolution, and is still predominant today. The desire for knowledge and erudition requires that we understand our surroundings.

To understand the present state of humanity and its prospects, we must build a bridge connecting several milestones in the evolution of science. These milestones have significantly affected our approach to life.

The Scientific Revolution that occurred during the 16<sup>th</sup> century brought radical changes in our thought patterns. At the time, researchers believed that theories must be tested against experiments and observations. They also cautioned us to avoid mythological and religious explanations. At the center of scientific thinking was an analysis of reality, and the search for scientific answers to age-old questions. Until then, these topics had been ascribed to a divine power.

In his book, *Mathematical Principles of Natural Philosophy* (1687), Isaac Newton (1642-1727) proposed a theory of mechanics that would let us calculate the change in the motion of any body when influenced by a given force. The success of Newton's theory presented a whole new worldview. Newton's deterministic viewpoint stated that in any event, regardless of its nature, a certain natural law will manifest. The presence of the Divine was of little importance because the trajectory of all motion is fixed, and there was no intervention by the Divine.

The deterministic approach was well described by the astronomer, Pierre Simon Laplace (1749-1827) as he sought to explain to Napoleon how our solar system had been formed. When Napoleon asked him about God's place in the process, Laplace replied: "Je n'avais pas besoin de cette hypothèse-là" ("I did not need this hypothesis there").

Thus, science left no room for the existence of other aspects beyond its own limits, including those realities that are hidden from our perception. Everyone believed that humanity had discovered the necessary measures to know the world as it really was.

In the late 1800s, it seemed that classical physics had provided researchers with a complete set of laws for every natural phenomenon. Many researchers maintained that these laws would help them explain even the few phenomena that remained mysteries. Since physics has always been considered "the mother of all sciences" and the forefront of technology and experimentation, its discoveries served as the foundation for research in other sciences, as well.

The era of modern physics began in the early 1900s with Albert Einstein's (1879-1955) revolutionary discoveries. Einstein's Theory of Relativity generated a fundamental change in attitude towards everything that had previously been known about time, space, mass, motion, and gravity. Einstein's theory unified time and space into a single entity—time-space—revoking the premise that time and space were absolute.

In the 1930s, another theory emerged: Quantum Mechanics, also known as Quantum Theory. This spurred an ongoing revolution in physics whereby all measurements yielded only approximate, quantitative results, probabilities that Quantum Theory calculations would interpret.

Quantum Theory was able to describe several phenomena that could not be explained by preceding theories. The most famous of these was wave-particle duality, showing that microscopic objects such as electrons behave as waves under some conditions, and as particles under others.

A fundamental concept of Quantum Theory is the Uncertainty Principle, which maintains that the *observer* affects the observed event. Hence, the key question is, "What do the measurements actually measure?" This principle implies that the concept of an "objective process" becomes irrelevant. Moreover, beyond the measured results, an "objective reality" simply cannot exist.

The discoveries of Quantum Physics drastically changed scientists' approach. The deterministic concept that maintained that physics revealed objective facts of nature and described their absolute existence was dismissed.

It was replaced by an understanding that physics does *not* know the true essence of nature. Physics can only assist in building paradigms, patterns, and formulae that calculate results of an experiment within a certain boundary of probabilities.

Contemporary science differentiates between the "actual reality" that exists independent of the observer, and the reality that the observer can describe. Today, researchers understand that what had once been defined as "absolute fact" is destined to give way to new conclusions and new experiments. These, in turn, will yield to ever-newer formulae and experiments.

It is now evident that science does not present the absolute truth, but rather a picture of the world as depicted through current experiments, perceptions, and paradigms. Moreover, the greater our knowledge of the world, the greater the uncertainties and contradictions we face.

Acknowledging the above has significantly diminished the predominance of natural science in general and physics in particular. Instead, it positioned science as a tool that uncovers a limited part of reality, rather than the absolute truth. The actual reality is hidden from us; we cannot discover it by means of scientific research.

In recent years, many scientists have become interested in various religions, new age theories, and mysticism. They are trying to find new tools and new ways to understand the hidden parts of reality, those unattainable by using conventional research methods.

This scientific predicament has escalated into a crisis since the turn of the century, challenging our ability to expose the full picture of the world we live in, and to understand the rules that govern both nature and humanity.

Once humanity exhausted its desire for knowledge and erudition and the visible reality had been researched, a new desire surfaced—to know the highest of concepts and the hidden part of reality. This is the stage of the evolution of desires that humanity has reached today.

This is the background for the appearance of the wisdom of Kabbalah, which offers humanity a new perspective, a scientific worldview that Kabbalists discovered thousands of years ago. Our current desire to know all of reality shows that humanity is ready to be exposed to Kabbalah.

The Kabbalistic perception of the world includes premises that other religions accept on faith, coupled with a scientific approach. Kabbalah develops tools within us that welcome us into a comprehensive reality and provide means to research it.

*Kabbalah, Science and the Meaning of Life* presents the fundamentals of the science that explores the aspects of reality hidden from scientists. When we discover those hidden parts, our knowledge of the world we live in will be complete. By uniting both the hidden and the revealed, we will prepare ourselves for accurate scientific research and the discovery of the genuine formulae.

By uncovering the hidden, our view of the world will become complete, liberated from the boundaries of relative perception and we will be able to unveil the existence of every part of reality, beyond time, space and motion. The Wisdom of Kabbalah grants all the above to anyone who truly seeks it.

This book is based on talks given by the author and compiled by his students.

# Kabbalah
## Meets
## Quantum Physics

A unique scientific conference was held in San Francisco, California in March, 2005, introducing Kabbalist Rav Michael Laitman, PhD and quantum physicists William Tiller, PhD, Dr. Jeffrey Satinover, and Fred Alan Wolf, PhD. All three scientists participated in the docudrama hit, *What the Bleep Do We Know?* The theme of the conference was "Quantum Physics Meets Kabbalah."

This fascinating conference consisted of intense closed discussions and public presentations. Following the introduction of the participants, Dr. Laitman gave an overview of Kabbalah, explaining the structure of reality and how the substance of Creation—the desire to receive pleasure—evolves. It only took one session to create a common language among the scientists.

Later that evening, the scientists presented their specific fields of expertise in a public panel before lecturers and students from the University of California, Berkeley, and Stanford University.

The next morning they returned to the discussion table. In between discussions they shared their impressions from the conference and exchanged stories of their own personal quests.

A few weeks later, Dr. Satinover attended an international congress in Israel whose theme was "The Wisdom of Kabbalah." During the congress, Dr. Laitman and Dr. Satinover discussed diverse topics such as freedom of choice, the global crisis, the family unit in the 21st century, the intensifying search for spirituality, and the future of humankind. Dr. Satinover gave a public presentation about quantum physics and its far-reaching implications.

The explanations of Kabbalah in this part of the book are based on these meetings.

The Editor

# ATTENDEES
# OF THE SAN FRANCISCO CONFERENCE

## PROFESSOR WILLIAM TILLER

Prof. William Tiller, PhD in Physics, University of Toronto, is a former Materials Science and Engineering Professor at Stanford University. He has published more than 250 scientific publications, including several books. His primary books are *Some Science Adventures with Real Magic; Conscious Acts of Creation: The Emergence of A New Physics; Science and Human Transformation: Subtle Energies, Intentionality and Consciousness.*

## FRED ALAN WOLF, PHD

Fred Alan Wolf, PhD in Theoretical Physics from UCLA, is a lecturer and a quantum physicist who has had contacts with renowned physicist David Bohm (1917-1992) and studied with Richard Feynman (1918-1988), among the most prominent physicists of the 20th century.

Dr. Wolf has also authored eleven books that were translated into several languages. Among his books are: *Taking the Quantum Leap: The New Physics For NonScientists; The Yoga of Time Travel: How the Mind Can Defeat Time; Matter into Feeling: A New Alchemy Of Science and Spirit,* and *Mind into Matter.*

## JEFFREY SATINOVER, MD, MSC

Dr. Jeffrey Satinover holds degrees from M.I.T. (SB), Harvard (EdM), the University of Texas (MD), and Yale (MS). He completed psychoanalytic training at the C.G. Jung Institute of Zürich. He is a former Fellow in Psychiatry and Child Psychiatry at Yale, where he was twice awarded the Department of Psychiatry's Seymour Lustman Residency Research Prize (2nd place). He was the 1975 William James Lecturer at Harvard. Until recently, he was a teaching fellow in the Department of Physics at Yale University. Today, Dr. Satinover is completing his PhD in Quantum Physics at Nice University in France and teaches constitutional law at Princeton University.

Dr. Satinover has written five successful books that were translated into nine languages and sold hundreds of thousands of copies. His most famous book, *The Quantum Brain*, set new standards in popular science writing and was celebrated by critics. This book touches upon several themes: mathematics, science, computers, quantum physics, and artificial intelligence. Two other books of Satinover's became bestsellers: *Cracking the Bible Code*, and *Homosexuality and the Politics of Truth*.

## MICHAEL LAITMAN, PHD

Rav Michael Laitman has a PhD in Philosophy from the Russian Academy of Science and an MSc in Bio-Cybernetics from the Polytechnic Institute of St. Petersburg. He was the disciple and personal assistant to Rabbi Baruch Ashlag (1907-1991) for twelve years. During those years, Rav Laitman acquired The Sulam Method, teachings passed on to his mentor by his father, Rabbi Yehuda Ashlag (1884-1954), known as Baal HaSulam for his *Sulam* commentary on *The Zohar*.

Rav Laitman has written thirty books on Kabbalah, which were translated into ten languages. His daily lessons are broadcast live and recorded on cable television in the US, in Israel, and on the Internet to tens of thousands of students worldwide. In recent years, Rav Laitman has become a frequent speaker at scientific conferences and conventions in Europe, East Asia and North America, expounding on the links between Kabbalah and science.

Dr. Laitman says that when he finished school, he was searching for a profession that would enable him to explore the meaning of life. He chose bio-cybernetics because this field researches life systems and the laws that dictate their existence.

"I had hoped," he explains, "that through this study, I would understand how the inanimate evolves to vegetative and then to animate. Yet the question that troubled me most was, "What are we living for?" It is a question that arises in each of us, but dissolves in the course of our routine race of life.

"When I completed my academic studies, I worked at The Leningrad Institute of Hematology in Russia. Even while conducting research as a student, I was fascinated with the wondrous way in which a living cell sustains life. I was awestruck by the harmonious incorporation of each cell in the body. The research centered around cell structures and their various functions in the body, but I could not find an answer to the question about why the entire body exists.

"I assumed that much like a cell in a body, the body, too, is part of a greater system in which it functions as a part of a whole. Yet, my attempts to research that question in the scientific framework were met with recurring rejections. I was told that science does not deal with these questions.

"Disillusioned, I had resolved to leave Russia as quickly as possible, hoping to continue in Israel the research that had so captured my heart. In 1974, after four years of being a 'refusenik' (a person who is denied an exit permit from the Soviet Union by the government), I received the longed-for exit permit and arrived in Israel. Alas, here, too, I was only offered to conduct studies and research on the limited single-cell level.

"I realized I had to search for a place where I could study the general systems of reality. I turned to philosophy, but before long realized that the answer was not to be found there. I then tried to find answers in religion, but had found nothing but a mechanical performance of The Commandments. There was no deeper understanding there.

"Only after many years of searching did I finally find my teacher, Rabbi Baruch Ashlag. I was with him for twelve years, from 1979 to 1991. To me, he was the Last of the Mohicans, the last Kabbalist in the chain of great Kabbalists that extended through the generations. I was his personal assistant and his disciple. I did not leave his side all through that period, and I wrote and published my first three books with his support in 1983.

"After my teacher passed away, I began to develop and publish the knowledge I had received from him. I considered it a direct continuation of his work. In 1991, I founded Bnei Baruch, a group of Kabbalists who study and practice the method of Baal HaSulam and his son, Rabbi Baruch Ashlag."

Since then, Bnei Baruch has become an international organization comprising many thousands of students. Its members research, study and disseminate Kabbalah.

Bnei Baruch maintains the largest Internet site on Kabbalah, offering a wealth of information in twenty-two languages, and the most extensive media and text archive of lessons, books, and films on the Internet. All the material is offered free through the site (www.kabbalah.info). Bnei Baruch recently established the Ari Films production company, producing documentaries and educational films aired on cable television networks in Israel, North America, and Europe.

Additionally, Bnei Baruch established the Ashlag Research Institute (ARI), named after Baruch Ashlag, which serves as a center for public discussions on Kabbalah. The educational and academic goals of the ARI derive from a deep commitment to bring the teachings of Baal HaSulam to the center stage of public discussion.

When Rav. Laitman saw the film, *What the Bleep Do We Know?*, he said: "I was overjoyed by the sensation that the scientists appearing in it were asking the same questions I once did. I thought that perhaps they would take interest in the wisdom Kabbalah offers."

# PRESENTING KABBALAH

An abbreviation of Dr. Laitman's presentation
at the public panel before students and teachers
from the universities of Berkeley and Stanford.

The wisdom of Kabbalah ("reception" in Hebrew), as its name implies, teaches us how to receive. It explains how we perceive our surrounding reality. To understand who we are, we must first learn how we come to sense reality around us, and how to cope with the events that befall us. The wisdom of Kabbalah provides us with all these insights.

The wisdom of Kabbalah does not come to an individual naturally, but only when one reaches the right level of ripeness. This is why Kabbalah is being exposed to so many these days, and this is also the reason why it was hidden for thousands of years.

Previous generations believed that the world exists by itself, whether or not we are there to perceive it, the world is the way it is and exists objectively, independently. Afterwards, people began to understand that our picture of the world is shaped by who we are. In other words, the picture of the world is a combination of our own attributes and external circumstances.

Therefore, we perceive only a part of everything around us. For example, right now there are numerous waves outside us, but we can only perceive one of them, the wave that we are attuned to perceive. Hence, we perceive external conditions according to our internal qualities. If we have nothing in common with the outside world, we will not perceive or feel any of it.

Kabbalah speaks extensively of our perception of time, space, and motion. Why does it seem to us that reality expands, that it is at a certain distance from us? What is the source of our perpetual sense of movement and change? Is this a result of internal processes that we are experiencing, or does it exist regardless of them?

The more we progress in the study of our internal being, the more we find that our perception of reality depends on us. Once humankind sufficiently evolves in knowledge, science, and technology, we will be able to perceive what the wisdom of Kabbalah has to offer.

The wisdom of Kabbalah says that around us there is only "The Upper Light," a single force in a permanent, unchanging state. Nothing exists besides this Upper Light. In such a state, the words *existent* or *nonexistent* mean the same because we only measure changes. When there are no changes, there is nothing to measure.

Within each of us is a "gene," a bit of information that constantly evokes in us new sensations and emotions. We picture the world from within these sensations, which is where we derive the awareness that we exist. All these processes occur within us and design our perception of the outside world.

Actually, nothing exists outside of us, but our picture of reality appears *as if* it were outside of us. The concept I am presenting here was described by the greatest Kabbalists thousands of years ago, and is both fascinating and awesome in the richness of experiences it provides. It is written in *The Book of Zohar (The Book of Radiance)* that only when we understand that perception, experience it, and master it will we understand the writings in the Kabbalah books and in the *Zohar* itself.

Once we have recognized the limits of our perception, Kabbalah can teach us how to discover what really exists outside of us. Through Kabbalah, we can transcend our natural qualities, build new tools of sensation, and through them fully experience the external reality.

When we are liberated from the chains of our innate perceptions, we can discover a whole new world and begin to experience life's eternal, complete, and unbounded flow. We will be able to experience the forces that operate on reality as a single power, and events that seemed accidental to us, unexpected or incomprehensible will suddenly make sense.

For such people, the spiritual world can become a system of forces that stands behind our perceived reality, the forces that propel reality. It is similar to examining embroidery: from the front, it looks like any other picture, but from the back, you can see the threads that comprise the picture, and their interconnections. Discovering these threads and interconnections provides knowledge about ourselves and the world around us.

The wisdom of Kabbalah is appearing now because we are living in a special time: on the one hand, we have many ways to succeed at being happy, but on the other hand, we cannot seem to achieve it. Kabbalah does not repeal any other teachings or sciences. Nor does it challenge humanity's progress over the generations. It cherishes humankind's achievements, but as we come to the crest of these achievements, humanity is beginning to experience a growing need to sense the complete reality. This is the reason for the growing interest in Kabbalah today.

To reach this goal and to experience the spiritual world, we must cultivate within us identical qualities to those of the spiritual world. Everything we perceive in reality is through an equivalence of qualities. Therefore, we see and discover new things in the world according to the qualities within us.

As we mature, we acquire new qualities, both from our parents and from our surroundings. After absorbing them, we can use them to study our surrounding reality. We acquire many different kinds of attributes, some of which awaken in us naturally in time, and some that are acquired by the influence of our environment. However, some qualities cannot be acquired naturally, and must be developed within us through a special method.

The wisdom of Kabbalah builds such qualities. The act of studying authentic texts by genuine Kabbalists affect us as readers in a unique way, evoking subtle discernments. There are no other texts or methods in our world that can do so. The study of Kabbalah creates a special perception with which we can begin to see what appears to be "ordinary reality" from a new perspective.

We can compare it to looking at a stereogram (A picture in which the delineated objects have an appearance of solidity). When we look directly at the picture, it appears to be a medley of incomprehensible lines. But if we blur our gaze, we will be able to "penetrate" the picture and discover a rich, three-dimensional image.

The wisdom of Kabbalah acts on us in much the same way, helping us "capture" that picture. In fact, Kabbalah doesn't present anything new, but simply refocuses our gaze so we can begin to "see."

When a person begins to perceive the correct picture, and experiences the opening of the Upper World, this discovery is accompanied by the wondrous sensation of eternal life, and endless, boundless stream of pleasures. This is where our lives are leading us.

# THE NATURE OF MATTER

The Wisdom of Kabbalah has evolved over thousands of years and been disseminated among Kabbalists throughout history. I would like to briefly review the key points in this process.

- The first Kabbalist was Abraham the Patriarch (approximately 1,800 BCE). *Sefer Yetzira (The Book of Creation)* is ascribed to him.

- 500 years after Abraham, Moses wrote his *Book of Torah (The Pentateuch)*, around 1,350 BCE.

- In the 2nd century CE Rabbi Shimon Bar-Yochai wrote *Sefer ha Zohar (The Book of Splendor)*.

- Kabbalah thrived in the 16th century Israeli town of Safed, led by the Kabbalist Rabbi Yitzhak Luria Ashkenazi, the Ari (1534-1572). He presented his method in his books, and today the wisdom of Kabbalah is founded on the Lurianic Kabbalah (the Kabbalah of the Ari). Lurianic Kabbalah relates to Kabbalah as a science—there is no meditation, chanting, charms, amulets or magical drawings of letters.

- Rabbi Yehuda Ashlag (1884-1954), known as Baal HaSulam (owner of the ladder) for his *Sulam (Ladder)* commentary on *The Zohar*, paved the way for our generation. His writings enable all of us to connect to the ancient, authentic sources that the past giants left behind.

The Kabbalah that we study today contains the same knowledge that was passed on from Abraham through all the generations. I was privileged to spend twelve years beside Baal HaSulam's eldest son and successor, Kabbalist Rabbi Baruch Shalom Ashlag, and from him I received this knowledge.

The wisdom of Kabbalah is a method for discovering the hidden part of reality, that imperceptible realm of reality that our five senses cannot grasp. It develops another sense in us, one that perceives the reality that exists beyond our present perception.

Kabbalah says that the whole of reality consists of a substance called "the will to receive pleasure." This will to receive pleasure is essentially a desire to be filled with delight, enjoyment; it is what we so often refer to as "egoism." This will to receive operates on all levels of existence: still (inanimate), vegetative, animate, and speaking.

Although the will to receive is the substance of all reality, the desire in itself is neither matter nor atoms, which came later. Everything that was created, that exists as the basis of reality, is based on the desire to enjoy, an aspiration for pleasure. In each level of reality, this aspiration takes on different forms.

Every Kabbalist, without exception, from Abraham to the last great Kabbalist, Baal HaSulam, maintained that the entire substance of Creation consists of a desire to receive. Every Kabbalah book speaks of the same thing, and all Kabbalists are in agreement in that regard.

Kabbalists are people who attain the Upper World; they speak from tangible attainment, not from theory. The word, "attainment," refers to the ultimate degree of understanding. Let me make things easier to understand by using some drawings.

We said that the will to receive is the basis of Creation. It is created by the expansion of the Upper Light. (In Kabbalah, the term "Light" designates giving, bestowing, love; it is referred to as "the Creator"). Thus, the Light created the will to receive that wants to be filled with the Light. Hence, the will to receive is also called *Kli* (vessel/receptacle), see Figure 1.

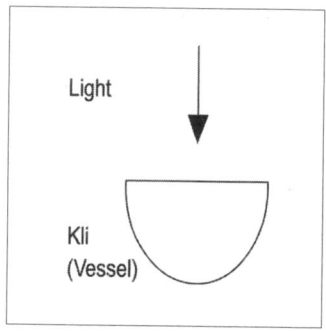

**Figure 1**

In other words, the desire to give creates the desire to receive, meaning the Light wants the *Kli* (vessel) to receive what it wants to give it.

The desire to enjoy is the beginning of matter; Kabbalah calls it "the primordial matter." However, it is still not a complete matter because at this point, it is created entirely by the Light's action. This process precedes the formation of any matter known to us, long before the material formation of our universe.

Since this will to receive stems from the Light's action, it senses the Light (the pleasure) at a very minimal level. At this point the will to receive has no independent desire for the Light. To make it independent and further develop the will to receive, we must add another element: the will's awareness of its own existence.

The Creator (Light) gives the will to receive the sensation that it exists, that there is "a Giver," meaning something that gives it the pleasure it is experiencing. Thus, once the will to receive senses pleasure, it begins to sense the giver of the pleasure within the pleasure.

Similarly, when we receive a gift, we feel the giver's attitude toward us beyond the gift itself. We should note that when we refer to the Creator, we actually refer to the giver. In this state of things, the created being (creature) begins to feel that there is a collision between the pleasure and the sensation of the giver of the pleasure (Figure 2). This collision stirs a reaction in the creature, making it want to be like the Creator because the Creator is higher than the pleasure itself. At this point, the will to receive evolves to the next degree.

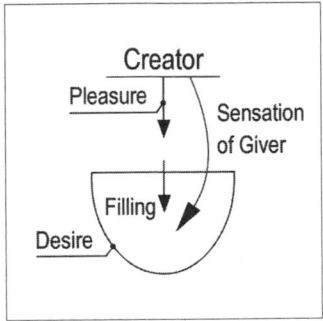

**Figure 2**

The will to receive then chooses to be a giver, like the Creator (the giver). This is the first reaction of the creature, though it is still not an entirely independent choice. It is rather a reaction that stems from its sensation of the giver, which makes it a compelled reaction, derived entirely from the presence of the giver. Thus, the will to receive has no free choice in the matter.

Now the creature begins to contemplate what it can give to the Creator. The Creator gives because He is the source of the pleasure. But when the creature wants to give as well, it finds that it has nothing to give in return.

Thus, through its need to give to the Creator, the creature discovers the nature of the Creator. The creature finds the

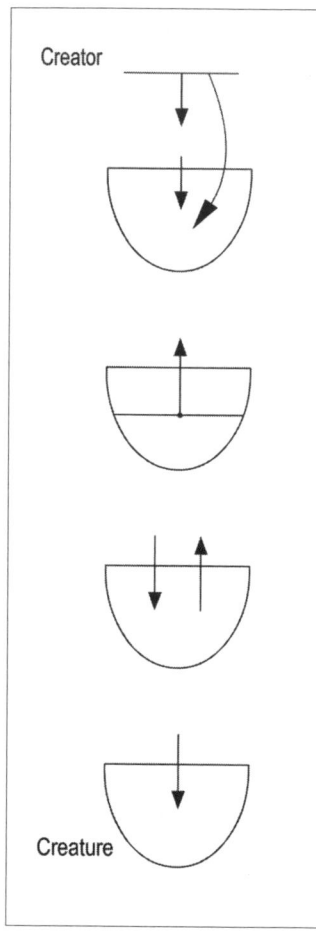

**Figure 3**

Creator's love for it. Yet, if the Creator loves the creature and wants to please it, it follows that the Creator should want or need something. The creature realizes that the Creator's need is His desire to delight the creature; when the creature enjoys, so does the Creator. But when the creature does not enjoy, neither does the Creator.

To realize its desire to give to the Creator as the Creator gives to the creature, the creature decides to receive the pleasure from the Creator. This process is somewhat similar to a child who eats to please its mother. In this way, even when the child receives food from its mother, it acts as a giver to its mother.

When the creature is in this state of being, we can say that it is similar to the Creator—it receives what the Creator wants to give, but only to give back to the Creator. The creature gives just as the Creator gives. However, this is not the end of the process. Now that the creature has performed a similar act to the Creator's, it experiences an additional pleasure—the pleasure of having the status of the giver.

This pleasure creates a new desire in the creature: a desire to enjoy the status of the giver, as well as the desire that the Light first created in the creature. This new desire does not come "from Above," and for that reason it merits the title, "a created being," "a creature" (Figure 3).

The root of the Hebrew word *Nivra* (created being) stems from the word *Bar* (outside). Thus, the term "creature" or "created being" refers to something or someone outside the Creator's will.

Once a creature is formed, it undergoes a sequence of interconnected states resulting from cause and effect. These states are referred to as "Upper Worlds." The Upper Light and the will to receive descend through the Upper Worlds to the lowest degree, called "our world."

At the degree of our world, we are totally controlled by the will to receive and we are completely detached from the sensation of the Upper Light, the Creator.

Once the will to receive descends to our world, it becomes independent from the Creator's domination because only by so detaching can the purpose of Creation--to make the will to receive identical to the Creator--be realized. In Kabbalah, this identical-ness is referred to as "Equivalence of Form between the creature and the Creator."

The wisdom of Kabbalah depicts each evolutionary stage of the will to receive from the very first stage of Creation down to our world. By studying these stages, we can understand how the material world, time, space, and motion were all formed, and how the will to receive will evolve.

Our entire history is determined by the evolution of our will to receive; this can help us understand how humanity evolves. Every process in reality, with no exception, is a result of our ever-growing will to receive.

Once the spiritual structure just described materializes, the matter that forms our world is created. Our world has experienced several evolutionary eras, and today we are at a stage where we are starting to understand that spiritual evolution must begin.

Today, humanity is facing a series of crises on both social and scientific fronts. Many signs point to today's bleak state of humankind and the global crisis it is experiencing. Drug abuse is perpetually increasing and begins at an increasingly younger age; depression is spreading like a plague, and international terrorism has become uncontrollable.

There is but one purpose to all of the above: to help humanity realize that the root of all our troubles is the intensification of our egoistic will to receive, and that we must mend it. Kabbalists wrote about the intensification of the ego ages ago, explaining that when humanity reaches this state, it will be time to disclose the wisdom of Kabbalah as a means to correct the ego.

Let's reiterate what we have discussed thus far. There is a Creator who wishes to give. This is the Root, or Zero Phase. In order to give, He must have someone to give to, and because the Creator wants to give, He creates a *Kli* that receives the "gift," meaning the Creator gives to the *Kli*. This is State One.

For this to occur, the receiver must first want the pleasure. If I build in you a desire for something and then give you what you want, you will not enjoy my gift because this is not your own desire. You must feel that it is your own desire before you can define it as "pleasure." Thus, at the end of State One, the creature begins to sense the Giver and His nature.

The will to receive evolves by sensing the Giver (State One), and consequently wanting to be like the Giver (State Two). In that state it becomes worthwhile for the creature to be like the Giver (State Three). However, this is only a phase in the formation of the will to receive, and the creature is not really aware that it is receiving anything.

In fact, the creature isn't aware of any of these observations; they are merely phases in the evolution of the crude will to receive. This crude desire must still descend, formulate, and drift far from the Creator until it stops sensing Him altogether. It must descend to the level of our world, and only then will it sense the desire in it as its own independent will (State Four). In this way, it will believe that it's free and does not submit to the Creator's guidance.

In this state, when an individual in our world wants to discover the Creator, the desire will seem to come first. Thus, a person will be able to give to the Creator out of free will, and this will constitute one's form of free giving. You might say that from the perspective of the Creator it is nothing but a fantasy, and that the Creator really runs the show. Although this is true, it does not diminish the fact that from the perspective of the creature, the concealment of the Creator enables the creature to feel independent.

At the end of State Three, the creature decides to receive from the Creator in order to resemble Him. Although in State Two the creature already has a desire to give, this is still not its own desire; this is not a "Creator-like" desire, as in State Three, but a desire that stems directly from the Creator.

Let me give you an example to explain what I mean. Assume that I am serving you a piece of cake. You might say that you don't know what this is, you have no initial craving for such a cake, but then I convince you that you really should try it because it's a fantastic cake. In this process I give you both the desire and the satisfaction, the fulfilling of the desire.

Therefore, there is an evolution in the transition between the stages where "this thing" (the craving) suddenly "wakes up" and becomes aware of itself. It is as though it begins to converse with the Creator. This evolution results from an interior collision in the creature between the two factors—the pleasure and the Giver of the pleasure. In reality, all that exists is these two elements.

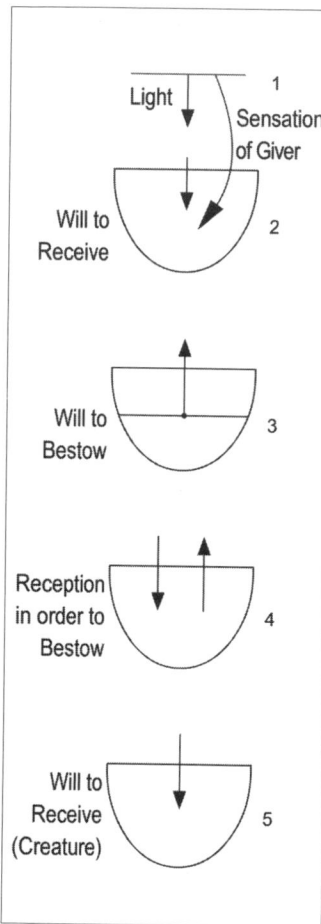

**Figure 4**

State Three also marks the awakening of a new desire in the creature: envy toward the Creator. In this respect, envy is a positive and useful element because it propels us to evolve further.

Finally, at the end of State Four, the creature feels that it is bringing pleasure to the Creator. Thus, it considers itself holding the same status as the Creator, and feels the pleasure that comes with having achieved the Creator's status, the pleasure from giving, from being a creator.

This state of being creates in the creature a desire to enjoy that status, relish in this pleasure. Because this desire does not come to the creature directly from the Creator, but evolves as a result of its own actions, it is considered a new desire, one that we ascribe to the creature. This is what we refer to as "the desire to enjoy" (Figure 4).

In this last state, the creature receives pleasure from sharing the Creator's status, and indulges in it. Thus, the creature indulges in two pleasures: the pleasure that comes from the Creator, and the pleasure that comes from sharing the Creator's status. This state of being is called *Ein Sof* (No End), and refers to a state where there are no limitations on the desire.

This does not refer to distance, time or space in the physical sense. Rather, this is an observation that pertains to the nature of the desire, meaning that the desire itself is unlimited.

Upon receiving these pleasures, the creature finds once more that there is a source of the pleasure. It discovers that the Giver is the source of the pleasure, and feels itself as the receiver. This time the sensation is valid because the will to receive in this state is the creature's own, not one that came to it from the Creator.

Consequently, the creature feels that it wants to escape its own desire. It shuns it, and does not want to belong to its own desire any longer. The rejection that it feels toward its own desire induces it to "restrict" it (avoid using it). The desire is still there, but now the creature refrains from using it. Hence, the sensation of fulfillment—the pleasure—ceases.

Having remained with a craving, the creature resolves to reach the status of the Creator, the only status that the creature now wishes to have—that of the Giver. It senses that it must give to the Creator without receiving any reward for itself. From this point onward, all its actions will be aimed solely to attain this goal.

To reach this objective, the creature executes a complex series of operations: It builds a chain of concealments (coverings) on the Upper Light, called "worlds" (the Hebrew word for "world" is *Olam*, which stems from the word *Haalama*, concealment). At the bottom of the chain of worlds stands "this world." Because the process that created the creature was comprised of five parts, the lessening of the Upper Light occurs through five degrees of concealment, five worlds whose names are *Adam Kadmon*, *Atzilut*, *Beria*, *Yetzira*, and *Assiya*.

In the process of constructing these worlds, the creature builds a surrounding environment for itself. In the world *Atzilut*, the will to receive is split in two: an inner part—soul—and an outer part—environment (surroundings), in which the soul operates. This stage still does not pertain to our world.

As a result of later events, the soul and its environment will experience a process of shattering, and consequently decline several degrees down to the degree of "this world." Only now begins the formulation of the matter that makes up our world.

From this stage onwards, from the broken will to receive, begins the historic evolution of the material world we are familiar with. Once the universe has been created, the still (inanimate), vegetative, and the animate degrees are made, and following them, the speaking (human) degree is formed (Figure 5).

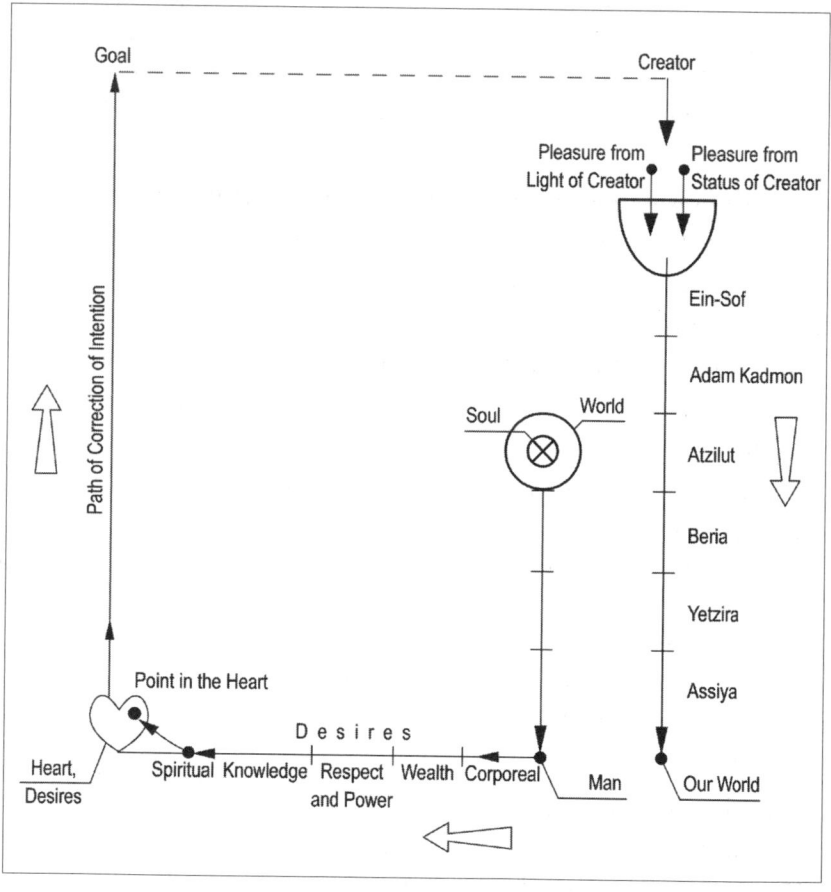

**Figure 5**

At its preliminary evolutionary stage, humanity has physical desires for sustenance, reproduction, and family. The body always has these elementary needs to sustain itself; we would need them even if we lived alone on an island.

The second stage in our evolution features a growing desire for wealth, followed by a desire for power and respect. These drives for wealth, power, and respect are considered "social desires," thus called for two reasons:

A) We absorb these desires from our social environment. Had we lived alone, we would not want them.

B) These desires can only be realized within a social framework.

The final evolutionary stage is the craving for knowledge and erudition. We want more and more knowledge, and want to know and research everything--hence the evolution of science.

Today, as we are nearing the conclusion of this evolution, which has taken us thousands of years, we are beginning to realize that it really did not yield anything. We find ourselves in a unique situation: we want to be filled with pleasures, but can't find around us any sources of true pleasure. Additionally, we cannot accurately define what it is we want. Thus, we find ourselves perplexed and disoriented, like lost children, not knowing which way to turn. Although we want something, we don't know what it is or where to find it.

We assign the word, "heart," to the sum of desires that have evolved in us through our life cycles: physical desires, social desires, and the desire for knowledge. Opposite these desires stands "the point in the heart," a "speck" of a new desire that evolves above all other desires. In fact, the point in the heart is the awakening desire to know the Upper Force, and it is the awakening of this desire that brings one to the wisdom of Kabbalah as a means to realize this desire.

The awakening of the point in the heart brings confusion, a by-product of this point's origins in the Upper World. The laws of the Upper World pertain to a reality where time, space, and motion do not apply.

Naturally, our brains are arranged so that we always think in terms of time, space, and motion. But in this new stage, we begin to feel that what determines everything is how we personally sense reality, and that reality in and of itself is unchanging.

Thus, we gradually come to sense that reality is static and that time, space, and motion don't really exist at all. We begin to realize that all our past experiences happened only within our sensations, that everything depends on how much we have cultivated our abilities to sense.

We need time to adjust to the concept that nothing changes except the measure by which we open our "tools of sensation." When we have done that, we will begin to sense the world we live in very naturally, simply, without any limitations, preconceptions, rules, oppression, coercion, or exterior pressures.

The point in the heart is the beginning of the desire for spirituality. Today, relatively few people are at this stage, but their numbers are increasing all the time. Eventually, every human being must come to the point where a craving for the Creator is uppermost, a point initiated by the above-mentioned envy, meaning the inherent need in every creature to reach the status of the Creator.

We must understand that when we said that the Creator is good, we meant that the Creator created us with the intention of bringing us to the best possible state of being, i.e. the Creator's own state. Hence, this is the state to which we must be brought. Any lesser state than this one will therefore not be considered adequate. It follows that the purpose of Creation is to allow us to reach the status of the Creator (see Figure 6, page 42).

In order to reach the level of the Creator, however, we must come to feel that our desire is totally opposite that of the Creator, that the Creator wants only to give, and that we want only to receive. This is the emptiness and darkness of the *Kli* (vessel) as opposed to the Light. Acknowledging this oppositeness builds us as creatures. For us to know the Creator, we must first know the opposite state from his, the "anti-Creator," a state of unbearable torments that poses a big question mark about our ability to endure these torments.

It is fair to say that we haven't yet begun the process of knowing the anti-Creator. To feel our complete oppositeness from the Creator, we will have to emotionally decline to much lower degrees. The wisdom of Kabbalah is surfacing now because it is impossible to experience these states physically, and Kabbalah is a means of easing our way through the states of oppositeness from the Creator, to experience them in our consciousness and our minds, not in our bodies.

We can compare this process to a person in pain. That person can either wait until the pain becomes intolerable and then turn to a physician, or turn to the doctor as soon as the pain appears. In the latter case, early diagnosis of the problem will spare one the suffering that comes with the actual breakout of the disease. In other words, a clever person takes medication as soon as symptoms of an illness appear, thus preventing its onset.

By so doing, one can evolve consciously, through reasoning, and thus the *Kli* (creature) learns to become aware of its oppositeness from the Light. The wisdom of Kabbalah is a method that helps us evolve through knowledge instead of through pain, and it is appearing today to allow humankind to acknowledge the evil that lies in egoism before it fully manifests itself, inflicting horrendous ruin in all aspects of life.

Hence, the wisdom of Kabbalah as the means to achieve both our evolution and the purpose of Creation should reach all of humanity. The more people engage in Kabbalah, and the more we circulate it throughout the world, the better off we will all be. Baal HaSulam writes about it very clearly in his *Introduction to the Book of Zohar.*

The first researcher to ask about the universe and the forces that conduct humanity was Abraham. He was one of many people who lived in Mesopotamia (ancient Persia), and in those days there was no division into nations. He discovered the method by which we can know the reality beyond our ordinary perception, and described his research and discoveries in his *Sefer Yetzira (Book of Creation).*

Abraham began to gather students and teach them the wisdom of Kabbalah. In time, this group of Kabbalists became a nation. Many years later, after the ruin of the First and Second Temples, this group of Kabbalists lost its perception of the Upper Reality; they fell from their degree of spiritual consciousness and were able only to perceive their physical reality.

This was actually a gradual process. Some lost their spiritual perception with the ruin of the First Temple, and the rest lost it with the ruin of the Second Temple. Rabbi Akiva was the last great Kabbalist to attain the degree of the spiritual law, "Love thy friend as thyself." The intensification of egoism induced unfounded hatred, and only religion remained for people, instead of the wisdom of Kabbalah.

Yet, despite the decline, a select few remained Kabbalists, and they passed the wisdom on from generation to generation until a time when all of humanity would need it. Today, we must rekindle the ancient science, revive the study of Kabbalah, discover the Upper Reality through it, and pass it on to all humanity.

It is important to note, however, that Kabbalah has nothing to do with religion, and does not imply that we need perform any physical actions. As we have mentioned previously, Kabbalah speaks only about desires and intentions with respect to the Creator.

This might lead us to conclude that, since the solution to our future challenges lies in the dissemination of Kabbalah to all humanity, we might have to convert everyone into Kabbalists. In truth, we don't have to.

Humanity is built like a pyramid. As in any other field of human engagement, ninety-nine percent of the world population is passive. They do not research or develop, but simply rely on the fruits of scientific discoveries.

Therefore, we should turn to those who are disturbed by the fate of our world and the future of humanity. We do not expect billions of people to study Kabbalah, but if we can use science to present humanity with the picture of reality, it will compel everything to change, as we are all parts of a single structure.

As we have said above, the *Kli* (vessel/creature) that the Creator created became a soul in the world *Atzilut*. This is the collective, or general soul, called *Adam ha Rishon* (The First Man). In the beginning, all its parts were bonded in wondrous harmony, and it was filled with the Upper Light. In that state, the sum of the parts created perfection. Later on, the soul experienced a process of shattering and fell to a degree called "below the barrier," where the spiritual sensation ends. The pieces of the single soul continue to exist below the barrier, but feel detached from one another (Figure 6).

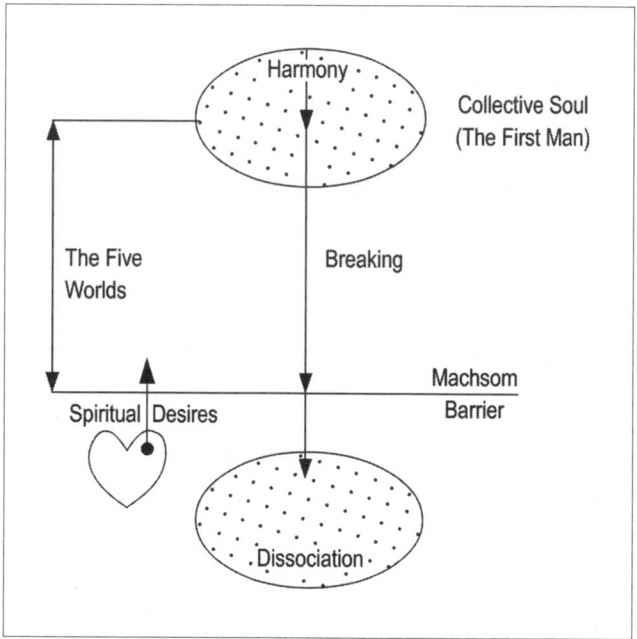

**Figure 6**

To clarify these words we can say that they remain in "the same place" as they were before, but another sensation is added to them. This is the sensation that they exist within themselves. In spirituality there are no places and the changes are merely in the quality of their perception and their sensations. Thus, each of the parts now lives within itself and senses nothing but itself.

Such a state of being is called "this world," which is the situation we are in today. The Upper Force is operating on us (the detached parts) to bring us back to the corrected state, and this will be the realization of the purpose of Creation.

Actually, the Upper Force "threw" us down to this world to acknowledge how different we are from It. We must come to want to rise back from this lowest point to the correct state of existence, where we are all connected. The gap between human nature and the Creator's nature is evident through millennia of sufferings, a complete process of descent and ascent designed to enable us to see how hateful we are to one another. In other words, every person's egoism must be exposed, and only then will we realize why we must willingly reconnect with one another.

We must understand the problem that arises when we want to satisfy a desire. For example, when a hungry person sits in a restaurant and waits for a meal, the minute the meal is served and the person begins to eat, the appetite begins to decrease. The more that person eats, the less hungry the person becomes, and with the lack of hunger, pleasure diminishes. Even if much of the food is left on the table, and even if the food is delicious, without a desire (appetite) for it, the pleasure ceases.

This scenario repeats itself in the fulfillment of every desire. If a desire appears in us, we are motivated to satisfy it. We strain and exert to fulfill our craving, but once we have achieved our desire, it vanishes. It might take a few minutes, a few hours or a few weeks, but sooner or later (mostly sooner) the fulfillment fades away. Thus, the same pleasure that satisfies the desire also eliminates it.

Moreover, obtaining one pleasure builds a desire that is twice as strong as before. Kabbalists have said that "One who has one hundred wants two hundred," one who has two hundred wants four hundred, and so on and so forth. As a consequence, when we obtain a certain pleasure, we remain twice as empty as before. If we could only find a way to always be filled with pleasures, we would be feeling eternal life.

There is one way to do this: to separate the "sensing unit" into two parts. One part will receive the pleasure, and the other part will sense it. In other words, if there were someone else to whom the pleasure would flow through me, my pleasure would not be quenched. If there were another person in the process of my receiving pleasure, the sensing unit would be split in two.

In such a case, I could separate the receiver of the pleasure from the one who feels it. The receiver would be another person, and the one who senses the pleasure would be me. In so doing, the sensing of the pleasure can become unending and yield a sensation of eternal living.

We can compare the above situation to a mother and her child. The mother enjoys her child's pleasure and can therefore give without restraint and delight in it. If I could love someone in such a way that pleasing him or her would feel like my own pleasure, my delight would be unlimited. In order to recognize that principle, our souls had to break and come down to this world.

When the point in the heart—a genuine desire to reawaken the sensation of the spiritual world—awakens in people, they come to the wisdom of Kabbalah. The study of the wisdom of Kabbalah is the study of our true state: the pre-shattering state. This is the only state that exists. Even now we are in it, though we are unaware of it. By wanting to come out of the dark state we are in and awaken to feel our real existence, we draw to ourselves the effect of the Light within that state.

Our efforts to unlock our tools of sensation and to perceive our actual state of being, develop new vessels in us. Thus we begin to feel how we are all connected as parts of a single system.

There is endless Light and fulfillment flowing continually through each part of the system. The reason for all the suffering and troubles the world is experiencing today is to force humanity to return to its true, perfect state, called *Gmar Tikkun* (The End of Correction).

Returning to the natural, perfect state is a process that the Creator has predetermined from beginning to end. Each phase is dictated from top to bottom. In each of us is a spiritual gene in which all our past, present, and future states are imprinted. The soul must move up the same route and stages from which it had fallen from Above. However, the way back depends on the extent to which we recognize that our egoistic state is bad, and our understanding that being closer to the Creator is the preferable state to experience.

Thus, the predetermined stages built in the spiritual gene evolve through the Light, namely through the Upper Force, and lead us from state to state. If we realize that it is in our interest to ascend and "invite" the Surrounding Light to work on us, we will accelerate our evolution and come to feel true spirituality. Hence, our freedom of choice lies only in accelerating the process.

The term "Surrounding Light" describes the Force that attracts us toward the attribute of bestowal. It draws us to the corrected state, which is the attribute of the Creator. All our future states exist within each and every one of us, even though we do not sense them. The projection of our altruistic, corrected state on our egoistic state awakens the attribute of bestowal in us.

As defined above, our corrected state is called Gmar Tikkun. At *Gmar Tikkun*, every soul is filled with boundless pleasures and a complete equivalence of Form with the Creator. In our present state, the Light that fills our souls at *Gmar Tikkun* shines in the form of Surrounding Light; its power is determined by the intensity of our desire to acquire the attribute of bestowal.

The Light is the power of bestowal, the power of giving. If a person wants to reach the attribute of bestowal, that person must make the force of bestowal—the light that fills one when he or she is corrected—project upon one's present state. The Surrounding Light corrects us and brings us back to the quality of bestowal. It is like a decent person who has gone astray and now reawakens to return to decency.

In fact, in order to cross the barrier that separates the corporeal world from the spiritual world, we must change our intention from relating to each other hatefully to relating to each other with love. The same rules apply to all parts of Creation, from the lowest element of reality to the highest. It all depends on the perspective of the observer who discovers the rules.

However, until a science is mathematically established, it cannot be considered a science. For example, quantum physics relates to a reality confined by time and space. But what we are talking about here is beyond time and space.

Hence, as long as quantum physics is not extended to include dimensions beyond time and space, it might be difficult for conventional science to proceed with the research. For this reason, it is important to find a tangential point, a connection between quantum physics and Kabbalah, for Kabbalah takes the research of reality to a place where physics cannot reach.

In other words, to progress to a higher level we must expand contemporary science to include consciousness, and this is a big step.

At this point, it might be beneficial to describe how Kabbalah relates to our perception of reality. We perceive reality through our five senses—sight, sound, smell, taste, and touch. However, all we really feel is our own reaction to whatever exists outside of us, with no perception of the actual, objective reality.

For example, a wave reaches my ear, which it interprets as sound. I know it because of the reaction of my ear's membrane to the wave that presses it. In truth, all I am measuring is my own reaction; I do not feel the wave itself. I perceive a range of sounds according to the changes in my hearing abilities and the health of my hearing mechanism. However, I have no idea what is actually happening outside of me. All our tools of perception and our senses work similarly.

We can say that we are closed in a box, and all that we measure is our interior impressions, creating in us a sensation that reality outside us changes. We cannot know if anything at all changes; we cannot even know if anything really exists outside of us. We simply have no means to come out of ourselves and test it.

Prof. Tiller mentioned Tor Norretranders, the renowned Danish researcher who published a book entitled *The User Illusion*. Norretranders notes an intriguing point regarding the functionality of the unconscious and what it contains. It appears that the five senses perceive fifty million bits of information per second, gathered as streams of information in the consciousness. The subconscious processes the information mathematically, but it only processes a tiny fragment of the information—some fifty bits of information per second.

Evidently, there is a huge gap between the received fifty million bits of information and the processed fifty bits. The important element to note is that the subconscious sends to the brain only the information that the brain determined in advance would be meaningful. The rest of the information is dismissed by the subconscious. These findings appear to corroborate the Kabbalah perspective with regard to the will to receive.

It is still unknown whether cutting-edge science and prominent researchers realize that the evolution of research depends on our changing our own interiors—the interior of the researcher. At the end of the day, we are studying ourselves; our ability to progress in research depends on the extent to which we change ourselves.

In the film *What the Bleep Do We Know?* and in similar publications of popular science, we can find claims that there are infinite possibilities around us. The wisdom of Kabbalah explains that all that exists around us is the Upper Light in a state of complete stillness, and all the changes and the endless possibilities are inside us. All that we see is the reflection of ourselves in the fixed, unchanging Light.

I regard the concept that to progress in research we must change ourselves as the next perception that the world will come to understand. It is a process that began with Newton, continued with Einstein, and continued with Quantum Physics. Now it is time for the next phase. Research will eventually discover that nothing changes except our inner tools, something that Kabbalists have discovered thousands of years ago. Today, a growing number of researchers and thinkers are anticipating that science will reach that view.

# THE GIVING FORCE AND THE RECEIVING FORCE

The Kabbalistic knowledge we possess is a result of Kabbalistic investigations performed by those people whose souls were burning with the question regarding the meaning of existence. They used a special method to begin to feel the comprehensive reality, and they wrote books about what they discovered. When Kabbalists first sense the complete reality, they call it "the opening of the eyes."

The opening of the eyes is a process of climbing up the same degrees by which we all came down from the previously mentioned infinite state (*Ein Sof*). The wisdom of Kabbalah comprises two parallel orders:

1. From Above downward—the descent of the will to receive from *Ein Sof* through all the Upper Worlds down to "this world."

2. From below Upward—the ascent of the researcher from this world, through the barrier, to the Upper Worlds, to *Ein Sof*.

Kabbalah talks about the will to receive, i.e., the desire to enjoy. As we have said, there are five stages in the creation process of the will to receive. We mark these stages with four Hebrew letters: the tip of the *Yod* (·), then *Yod* (י), *Hey* (ה), *Vav* (ו), *Hey* (ה), and for short we call this structure of letters *HaVaYaH*. We also assign these five stages five respective names: *Keter, Hochma, Bina, Zeir Anpin*, and *Malchut*.

The tip of the *Yod* is *Keter* (Figure 7), designating the beginning of the manifestation of the desire that departs from the Light, like a black dot inside the Light. From this dot evolves the letter *Yod*—the primordial desire. The shape of the letter *Yod* is like a point with a prickle at its head and a tail at its end. It symbolizes the creation of the new matter—previously nonexistent—the will to receive. This stage is called *Hochma*.

Once the letter *Yod* evolves, the will to receive continues to evolve by absorbing the attribute of bestowal from the Creator. The combination of the attribute of bestowal and the attribute of reception generates a new quality, called *Bina*, designated by the letter *Hey*.

*Bina* contains the first matter that wants to be similar to the Light that engendered it. The shape of the *Hey* symbolizes the integration of the attributes of reception and bestowal. This generates the form of bestowal atop the primordial desire.

Following that, the desire wants to perform an act of bestowal, as the Creator previously did, and therefore tries to be like the letter *Yod*. But because this time it is an act that the desire itself performs, it is assigned the form of the letter *Vav*.

The letter *Vav* symbolizes our efforts to be like the Giver, the Creator. However, the act of *Vav* is considered incomplete because it is a decision that was made beforehand, a consequence of *Hey*'s wish to bestow. The incompleteness of the desire, symbolized by the letter *Vav*, is hinted in its name *Zeir Anpin*—small face (Aramaic). *Zeir Anpin* lacks the independent decision, the "head."

When *Zeir Anpin* performs the act of bestowal, it discovers what it means to be a giver. In consequence, it begins to want to reach the status of the Giver, and this last desire is called *Malchut*. *Malchut*'s desire is aimed entirely toward receiving the attribute of bestowal, hence, like *Bina*, it is symbolized by the letter *Hey*.

However, there is a fundamental difference between the first *Hey* of *Bina* and the last *Hey* of *Malchut*. In *Bina*, the combination of reception and bestowal stems from the Creator, "from Above," while in *Malchut* this combination comes "from below," from our craving for the status of the giver, a desire that stems from its own will to receive. Now we can see why the letters *Yod, Hey, Vav, Hey* symbolize the name of the Creator. It is the pattern by which the Creator formed the will to receive, within which the will to receive senses the Creator as a Light that fills it.

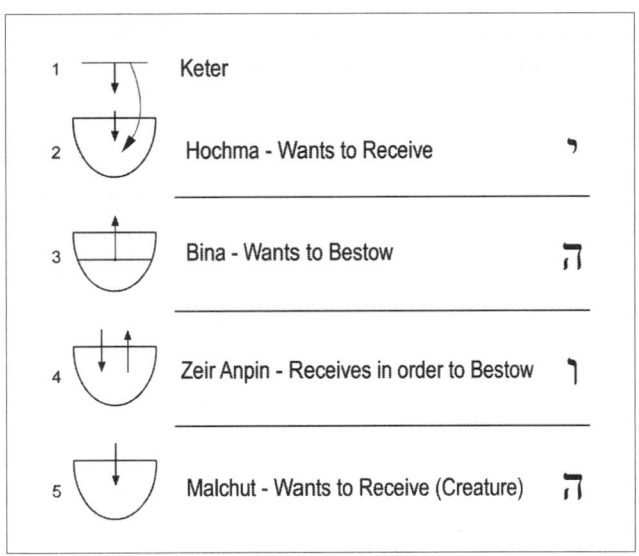

**Figure 7**

Once the Light filled the will to receive in *Hochma* and in-stilled it with the sensation of the Giver, the desire began to sense itself as a receiver, and wanted to become like the Giver. The de-sire can easily change its nature because at this stage, the desire is not an independent desire, but one that came from the Creator. However, the will to receive in *Malchut* is already an independent desire of the creature.

When the will to receive in *Malchut* wants to receive both the Light that comes from the Creator, and the pleasure of hav-ing the status of the Giver, it begins to see the oppositeness of its own attributes from those of the Light. The will to receive then experiences the gap between itself and the Light. Sensing this painful gap brings it to perform the *Tzimtzum* (restriction of Light). In other words, the reaction to discovering how opposite its attributes are from the Creator's, is removing all the Light that filled it.

From this stage onward, the *Tzimtzum* (restriction) becomes the governing law in all of the created being's actions. The Light will no longer enter an opposite desire from the Creator because the creature decided so. In this manner, the *Tzimtzum* becomes a binding law in Creation.

The law of *Tzimtzum* implies that as long as we (the creature) are egoistic, we will not be able to sense the Creator and the pleasure that comes from Him. There is only a tiny segment of the whole reality, called "this world," where one can receive pleasure and enjoy within an egoistic desire, despite the law of *Tzimtzum*. This enables us to exist on the physical level before we begin to correct ourselves and become more like the Creator.

We must understand that an egoistic existence, such as our current existence in this world, does not exist in reality. Ascending from this world implies the ascension of one's desire toward the quality of bestowal. In this world, the will to receive works inwardly, and in the spiritual world, it works outwardly, giving, like the Creator.

In other words, the spiritual world observes the law of *Tzimtzum*, and the term "spirituality" refers to states in which we are similar to the Creator. In our present state, we are egoists, and are opposite from the Creator.

Let us go back to the process of creation. The term "world" depicts a certain state of the creature, the will to receive. Thus, the state of the creature prior to the *Tzimtzum* is called "the world *Ein Sof*" (the infinite world), and its state following the *Tzimtzum* is called "the world of *Tzimtzum*" (the world of restriction).

After the *Tzimtzum*, the *Kli* (vessel/receptacle) remains empty and should decide what to do next. It feels that staying empty is pointless for both itself and the Creator. The act of the *Tzimtzum* made it independent of the domination of the Light, but by that it still did not come to anything because the *Tzimtzum* does not make it a giver like the Creator.

The *Kli* understands that it can carry out a similar action to the one it had performed while transiting from *Hochma* to *Bina*. However, this time it would be of its own free, independent will. It understands that it can give the Creator pleasure if it were to receive the Light from Him with the intention to give to Him. After all, this is the Creator's will—to delight and please the creature.

Thus, when the Light-pleasure reached the creature-*Kli*, along with the sensation that it came from the Creator, the creature first rejected them. It did that so it would not sense them directly and thus feel the shame of being opposite from the Creator. In this manner, the creature followed the law of *Tzimtzum* that does not allow reception for the sake of self-gratification.

Afterwards, the creature measured the pleasures before it and weighed the result against its own desire to enjoy. It received this specific amount of pleasure only after it knew exactly how much it could receive in order to please the Creator, and not to please itself. The rest of the Light was then repelled.

Kabbalists explain this by using the example of the guest and the host. The host serves all kinds of exquisite delicacies and ushers the guest to the table. The guest feels shame and declines politely. In truth, the guest is afraid to feel like a receiver, and hence guards his ego from shame.

Now it is the host's turn to implore: "I have made it all for you! You know how I care for you. I want to delight you with what I have prepared for you; please, will you eat for me?" By so doing, the host displays before the guest a deficiency, a need for the guest to receive. Now the guest feels that consenting to eat the food would fulfill the host's need. Eating would thus be doing the host good.

Thus, the balance of power changes: if the guest receives in order to please the host, it is no longer reception, but bestowal. It follows that the guest uses the host's love to give pleasure back to the host.

Another example of a giving-receiving relationship is between parents and children. Actually, the child is the head of the family, using the parents' love to manipulate them in order to satisfy its needs. Naturally, the people in these examples are egoists. Things happen quite differently in the spiritual world, but such examples can help us understand the principle. The process occurring in the Upper Worlds is built upon a very similar principle: if one receives pleasure for the sake of pleasing the Creator, it is not considered reception, but bestowal. In performing this act, the human being equalizes with the Creator and acquires the Creator's thoughts.

In other words, the Light created us from the very beginning with a massive, total desire for it. This desire is in us even now, but it is latent, and thus we do not feel the Creator's Light. This desire (for the Light) must be evoked.

It is important to realize that we are dealing with researching the term "Creator" in a purely scientific manner. In other words, we can measure our sensation of the Creator in precise tools, quantify each sensation, and express it numerically. The tool with which we measure the sensation of the Creator is called "the wisdom of Kabbalah." We can precisely define which Lights permeate which part of the *Kli*, how powerfully, and under which conditions.

Kabbalah talks about the will to receive created by the Creator. These two—the will to receive and the Creator—are much higher elements, in the sense that they precede all religions and belief systems. Kabbalah is about the two working forces of reality, the giving force, called "Creator," and the receiving force, called "creature."

Kabbalah has nothing to do with any religion or any faith. I do not want to compare Kabbalah to other teachings, nor do I wish to discuss any religion, be it Hinduism, Judaism, Christianity, or Islam. After all, why deal with religion when we can discuss the physics of the Upper World?

The challenge in explaining this material is that we cannot compare our emotions. We cannot say that the term, "Upper Force" that one person feels is identical to the term, "Upper Force" that another person feels. Hence, trying to compare this or that teaching to the Kabbalah is pointless.

Kabbalah is a technique that provides accurate, mathematical, measurable tools. When I document data pertaining to one state, another Kabbalist can perform the same act—with his or her own tools—and experience the data I was referring to. The wisdom of Kabbalah provides an accurate measurement of human emotions.

Kabbalah books describe the Kabbalists' impressions of the Upper Force. They describe their emotions and leave us with formulae that explain which internal actions we need to perform on our will to receive. In so doing, we learn how to perform acts of reception and bestowal of the Light that the Creator wants to impart to us.

A Kabbalist measures the pleasure that can be received or repelled very accurately. Thus, we are given exact instructions as to the type of inner work we must do at each stage. Thus, we will know how to work with our desire vis-à-vis the Light.

# BETWEEN KABBALAH AND SCIENCE

A talk with Dr. Jeffrey Satinover
and Michael Laitman, PhD,
Israel, April 2005

## THE CONCEPT OF FREEDOM IN QUANTUM PHYSICS

**Rav Laitman:** What is the existing outlook of science on the topic of freedom of choice?

**Dr. Satinover:** Modern science as a whole—and I'm using the term "as a whole" because I will shortly present a significant correction to it—perceives reality as mere *material* reality. It regards the material reality as whole, as a complex machine. I will demonstrate this concept using a toy-train model. If we switch on the train, it will ride the rails and little people will move about in it. This model is only a machine.

You will certainly say that in the toy-train model, each of its parts has no freedom of choice. Similarly, most contemporary scientists will tell you that the physical universe is exactly like the toy train, and that every action of each part in the universe is determined entirely by preceding events in the universe. They will even insist that there is no other model. Reality is made solely of a universe and a "toy train" within it; there is no builder, no engineer who designs and builds the toy train.

Alongside this view, there is a branch of modern science called "Quantum Mechanics." This branch acknowledges that the theory we just presented is incorrect, and that there is in fact an element of complete freedom in the physical universe where particles of atoms do not behave mechanically, but "choose" how to behave. I am using the word "choose" in quotation marks because our language is too limited to explain it sufficiently. The real problem is that science cannot say anything about the nature of whatever makes those choices, hence they appear utterly random to us.

If one properly understands quantum theory—the most advanced of sciences—one can see that there is a possibility of genuine free will in humans. However, modern science cannot clearly explain how and where such free will is used.

**Rav Laitman:** It seems that beyond ordinary and accessible nature, particles have some way of "choosing freely," but how does this affect human beings? All this does not imply that we have free choice in day-to-day life. Perhaps, somewhere, in the depth of matter, there are additional forces or probabilities that adhere to a regularity that we cannot conceive of in the ordinary determinism.

**Dr. Satinover:** Correct. These are subtle and complex discernments. The greatest minds of science have been arguing over them for the past eighty years. It appears that single electrons, despite their limitations, can "freely elect" from several trajectories. Electrons cannot do much; they cannot write books, marry, or go to war. Nonetheless, within their limitations, it appears that they do have a certain measure of freedom.

When I say that "the electron chooses," I am using rather loose phrasing. The truth is, we don't really know who or what makes the choice. What we do know is that the behavior of every particle of matter in the universe is twofold: in part, it behaves according to fixed laws, and in part, it behaves irregularly, affected by something that is not a part of our known universe.

Thus, one might say that, for instance, the creation of our universe is also twofold—in part, a result of prior physical processes, and in part, created by an Upper Force. But science cannot prove this. All it can prove is that we understand that physical actions are not determined solely by the physical actions that precede them. Rather, we understand that "something else" affects matter, but science cannot tell us what that something is, and certainly not how to research, confirm, or rebut it.

Some might argue that it is as though electrons had pseudo-brains of their own that make those decisions, but I do not endorse this theory. At this point, you are free to believe whatever you choose.

When a quantum object connects with another quantum object, it sets off the decision making process, ignited by the connection between them. This process can be with an observer who is watching the particle, but the observer is not mandatory.

The true mystery is not in the question of the external observer, but in the fact that there seems to be some latitude passed on within matter. That latitude points to "something" that is beyond the material universe, without telling us anything about the nature of that "something."

**Rav Laitman:** I cannot see why we haven't encountered this mystery thus far. When we research the human body and human psychology, we do not find any latent forces that cause unexplained behaviors. It is odd that we had to split atoms to the tiniest particles to eventually find that there is nothing in them but a tiny energy burst where we finally see that we don't know where they will move in an instant, or even if we are facing a wave or a particle. Would it not make more sense to first find these hidden forces at a much higher level, one that pertains to human consciousness? Why is it that physicists, who study lifeless atoms, are the ones that suddenly find a hidden life among these particles?

**Dr. Satinover:** I think that this is one of the great ironies of the 20th century. Newtonian physics discovered a lifeless universe. The view that matter is lifeless, and perceiving it as a mere machine evolved as an offshoot of research in physics, chemistry, and biology. Eventually, physicists produced a perception that humans are nothing but machines, as well.

On a day-to-day level, intuitively and emotionally, we experience ourselves as free creatures that make our own choices. Moreover, psychologists rely on the premise that their patients can choose freely. If I thought of my patients as machines, I would give up my practice as a psychologist.

Nonetheless, the reasonable and rigorous premise from the beginning of the 17th century up to the 20th century, a premise that all sciences relied on, is that all things are machines.

It is true that most people do not feel like machines in their daily lives, hence the inconsistency between the scientific worldview and the way people actually lead their lives. Modern medicine, modern psychiatry, and all the doctrines that research the human mind and nervous system leave no room for the assumption that people have free will.

**Rav Laitman:** What you are saying implies that physicists, too, did not want to cope with a non-mechanical system. Yet, the discoveries that arose from the experiments forced us to acknowledge that there is another force that abrogates the deterministic results we had anticipated.

**Dr. Satinover:** This is just what happened. It was evident only when rigorous experiments in quantum mechanics were executed at the subatomic level. The first results left the scientists dumbfounded. Einstein, for instance, supported the view that the world was a lifeless machine. He thought that quantum mechanics was impossible and even defined it as "insane." The possibility that there might exist any freedom in matter made him proclaim his well-known assertion: "God does not play dice with the universe."

Although Einstein used the word "God," he was using that word cynically. What he meant was that at this level of matter, there cannot be any freedom such as the experiments demonstrated. He realized that if freedom existed at this level in matter, it would mean the end of science, which is why he said that science cannot be structured upon such postures.

**Rav Laitman:** Why does that have to mean the end of science? Hasn't scientific research always impelled us to progress and to change our views? Why are so many scientists saying that we are approaching the end of science?

**Dr. Satinover:** First, Einstein was wrong when he thought that this would be the end of science. He was also wrong when he thought that quantum mechanics is false. Quantum mechanics research showed that scientific knowledge has its limits. Scientists of quantum theory reached the boundary of research and then left it.

I believe that the most important fact concerning your expertise is that quantum theory makes it very clear that there is a limit to science's ability to know, and at the same time points out that there is "something else" on the other side of the boundary. I have noticed that many people miss that point, and get mixed up between quantum theory and Kabbalah. Quantum theory states unequivocally that science *can* reach that limit and prove that it exists, but quantum theory also says that science *cannot* say anything about what lies beyond that boundary. This is not in the hands of science to discover, and at this point, science admits its limitations.

**Rav Laitman:** Our perception of reality stems from our research of reality. It is created within us according to our senses and our perception. Quite possibly, if we had been created with mental and intellectual technologies that let us analyze what we see differently, we could cross that border. In other words, while this may be the limit of our present qualities, perhaps this limitation exists only in our present state. Is it possible that we could find some way to change our attributes and cross that boundary?

Let me put it differently: Is it possible that everything we do not know about quantum particles stems from the fact that we are caged within a framework of time, space, and motion? Were we somehow liberated from this boundary, could we have seen the whole process differently? Would the unknown become known if we improved our qualities?

**Dr. Satinover:** In this talk, I deliberately chose to leave my personal view of the world, of spirituality and of Kabbalah aside. I am not an expert on any of them. Here I am trying to serve as an emissary of the scientific world and remain self-effacing concerning what science can or cannot do.

It is possible that human beings were emanated as creatures of spiritual potential that enables them to cross that border. As a human being, I long to do just that, and I think that all people will strive to this. It might be that Kabbalah is the scientific method that makes doing that possible.

Yet, hard science requires us to be vigilant and to recognize its limits. Science can lead humankind to the borderline, but it cannot take us across. In other words, a scientist cannot use quantum theory as a method to cross the border that the method itself points to.

**Rav Laitman:** Concerning the argument that there are infinite possibilities around us, is it not the observing scientist who chooses from among them?

**Dr. Satinover:** We do not know. Quantum theory demonstrates that certain particles choose one trajectory and others choose another; but we cannot say where this choice comes from. Nothing can be said about it from a scientific point of view; it is a complete mystery.

The trick is to recognize the mystery, not to pretend that we have an answer when we don't. Such recognition can prompt us to realize that there is a "beyond" to reality. This recognition does not tell us what it is, but it can bring us to start wondering about it.

## THE FAMILY UNIT

**Dr. Satinover:** What is the Kabbalistic approach to relationships between men and women at the start of the 21st century and what is the Kabbalistic prognosis in that field?

**Rav Laitman:** From the perspective of Kabbalah, it is important that a man and a woman be together, marching together on the path of self-correction and reaching congruence with the Upper Force. By doing that, they will complement one another on both material and spiritual levels. Both the man and the woman have certain corrections to make. By making their personal and reciprocal corrections, they will come to the right connection in such a way that their relationship will resemble the Upper Force.

The difference between what is happening in the 21st century compared to what happened throughout history is that today we are involved in a comprehensive crisis. This crisis is evident in every field of human engagement, including personal and familial.

Its cause is the intensification of the ego and the desire to indulge in pleasure. Today, human ego is at its apex; we can no longer control it. As a result, we are losing the ability we once had to cope with ourselves and our world.

We no longer want to belong to each other or to a family. As the ego runs amuck, people cannot stand to be near one another. Family relationships in general, and spousal relationships in particular, are the first to be harmed by the ego's outburst, as our spouses are the closest people to us.

In the past, the family was sheltered from fluctuations—it was an island of stability. When there were troubles in the world, we left home and fought, but longed to return to it. When we had troubles with our neighbors, we could relocate, but our family unit was always considered a safe haven. Even when we did not really want a family, we kept the family unit alive to care for our children or elder parents.

Today, however, the ego has grown so much that nothing can contain it. We keep trying to handle our egos and fail repeatedly. It is true that in some places, the situation is not yet so extreme. However, this will soon change, due to the awakening of the ego throughout the globe.

The solution to this problem is to begin correcting our nature—correction of our egos. If we do nothing to correct our egos, we will all plunge into drug abuse or suicide, or experience the violence of global terrorism. We will certainly not want to have children or raise families, a trend we are already seeing. Even without ecological catastrophes, we will decline into chaos and self-destruction. Our present situation requires that we ask ourselves what we are truly living for, and if there is a way out of our plight.

This is the point where we arrive at the wisdom of Kabbalah. Kabbalists have written that at times such as ours, the Kabbalah will surface to help us correct our nature. We can thus use Kabbalah to rise to a new level of eternal and complete existence.

## PERSONAL FATE AND COLLECTIVE FATE

**Dr. Satinover:** What is the Kabbalistic explanation of personal fate and collective fate? I understand the importance of unity among people, but does Kabbalah have a position concerning each individual regardless of the fate of others?

**Rav Laitman:** The wisdom of Kabbalah specifically promotes personal growth. We can demonstrate it through the Kabbalistic approach to education; Kabbalah maintains that the proper education is achieved solely by means of personal example. It is pointless to try dictating to people.

Proper rearing is based on building a correct, effective environment in addition to providing good personal examples. People will act according to the examples they observe and use them according to their personal level of evolvement. We must treat every person according to his or her individual strength, since everyone in the world is unique.

All of us are segments of one collective soul, and each of us possesses a unique part of the whole. If even one part of the general soul is absent, the structure will be incomplete and we will not reach the purpose of Creation. Hence, we must cherish the personal part of each and every person. We must allow everyone to evolve in a way suitable for them to flourish.

Kabbalah distinguishes between a proper social life and personal, individual evolution. To sustain society, everyone must certainly adhere to the rules it has set. But when it comes to personal growth, the uniqueness of every person must be fervently guarded. Kabbalah explains in great detail how personal growth and adherence to society's rules should be intermingled, and specifies how to build a correct society that allows for all of its members to evolve in their own unique way.

Kabbalah strictly objects to any cultural or educational coercion from Western countries toward third-world countries. This is harmful to both. Coercion ruins the uniqueness of these peoples because it does not let them evolve at their own pace and according to their own rules and culture. This situation is creating a real deformity within humankind and producing deplorable results.

## THE *TZADIK* (RIGHTEOUS)

**Dr Satinover:** What is the nature and role of the *Tzadik* (righteous person)?

**Rav Laitman:** The term *Tzadik* refers to a person who is at a degree where he or she *Matzdik* (justifies) the actions of the Upper Force. The *Tzadik* justifies everything that happens in Creation because he or she has come to sense the whole of Creation, not just the part accessible to our five senses. The righteous sees the rules that govern the realm beyond the boundaries of our five senses—the rules that affect our world, create everything within it, govern the unfolding of every event, and lead it to the purpose desired by the Creator.

Thus, clearly a *Tzadik* is a Kabbalist, one who discovers the Upper World, the World of Forces, the level at which plans concerning this world are made, and from which they come down to operate it.

The nature of the *Tzadik* corresponds to the level the individual *Tzadik* has reached. Kabbalah explains that all that we feel in reality adheres to the principle of "equivalence of Form," the "congruence principle."

In each of our five senses, we perceive a certain span of reality. For example, our sense of hearing enables us to hear a certain range of frequencies, and our eyes can see a finite range of colors. If we had additional senses, we could perceive reality differently and perhaps perceive additional dimensions.

Actually, we cannot even imagine how we would perceive reality if we had other senses. It turns out that our five senses with their specific spans create limits defining our sense of reality. We cannot exceed this limit.

There is, however, a method that allows for perception beyond this picture of reality, including the forces that govern our reality, which we call "the Upper World." The way we are able to perceive them is based on the same principle that applies to our perception of reality, namely "equivalence of Form." In other words, we must match ourselves to these forces.

Our task is to cultivate the attributes that inhabit the Upper Sphere, which conducts our world. However, it is impossible to know these attributes before we reach them. Hence, here we are assisted by Kabbalists, those who are already "there," who teach us how to acquire these attributes. They explain how one can develop an additional, internal sense, a "soul," through special activities. Using that sense, we can perceive an additional reality that was previously hidden; hence the epithet of Kabbalah—"the wisdom of the hidden."

Perceiving that hidden reality brings us to understand the formulae by which it operates us, the goal to which it is leading us, and the way in which it is executing these formulae. The Kabbalist is inside that reality and is an integrated part of it, a part that justifies it. In that state, a person is called a *Tzadik*, and this is the *Tzadik*'s nature.

125 degrees comprise the justification of the Creator's actions. Total agreement with the Creator's actions is achieved at the last degree. Every person must reach this final degree. This process of life and death, which repeatedly "recycles" us to this world, is what enables us to rise to the degree of utter righteousness, that of one who completely justifies the Creator.

## HUMAN SUFFERING

**Dr Satinover:** I think the topic that people find most difficult to accept is human suffering. On the one hand, suffering motivates people to search for spirituality. On the other hand, it is very hard to accept suffering. How does Kabbalah relate to this question?

**Rav Laitman:** This is indeed a question that troubles everyone. On the one hand, we are speaking of a benevolent Upper Force, but if it is "Upper," it means it is better than us. Yet our world is filled with anguish and torment. Do anguish and torment also come from this Force? Is there more than one Force, and if so, are they at war with each other?

**Satinover:** I am referring not only to the philosophical question of the nature of suffering, but also to the practical aspect.

**Laitman:** Reality is made of our desire to enjoy and the pleasure that motivates this desire to operate. These are the only two components on all levels of reality—the pleasure and the desire to receive pleasure. In Kabbalistic terms we call them "the Light and the Kli (vessel)."

When pleasure is absent, it creates a sensation of a desire to enjoy. But sometimes the deficiency of pleasure is so intense that it creates a sensation of suffering. Because everything is made of a certain measure and quality of a desire to receive pleasure, everything also suffers when it is absent—minerals, plants, animals, and people.

In fact, suffering is a necessary sensation that impels a creature to leave its present state and move on to the next. Without suffering, there is no motion. In fact, motion means that my present state is unsatisfactory, so I decide that I will be better off in a different state. Suffering enables us to make the necessary effort to move toward a situation that seems better. Hence, without suffering, progress is impossible.

The Upper Force has no other way of promoting us to better states except through suffering. If it created us as egoists with a desire to indulge in pleasure, then the only way it can move us from one state to the next is through a sensation of suffering.

However, we still need to explain why there is so much more suffering today than before. The purpose of Creation is for humankind to reach the highest degree in reality.

The only way to approach that goal is with an immense drive to reach it, or phrased differently—from the greatest suffering. This does not necessarily relate to physical suffering. We seemingly have everything today, yet we feel that something is missing, and that sensation of absence is the greatest degree of suffering.

To advance, to exit the boundaries of this world and begin to search for something higher, we must suffer. We must feel suffering at the deepest level so that we can demand the correspondingly highest state. That sublime state of being that stands vis-à-vis this world is the spiritual world; hence the suffering, too, must be spiritual, not physical.

In spiritual suffering, one does not suffer from absence of mundane fulfillments. While mundane fulfillments exist, they do not provide a sensation of livelihood, or even a sensation of being alive. Those who specifically regret a lack of "feeling alive" will have the strength to ask for something beyond this life.

For this reason, we are not going to see a satisfied humankind in the near future. On the contrary, suffering will intensify and will take on a more spiritual form. The sensation of absence of spiritual fulfillment will overshadow any physical abundance. There will be nothing satisfying and nothing joyful for us. Depression will spread throughout the world and the sensation of distress will not let us live our lives in peace.

The result of this distress will be an increase in conflicts, terror, outbreaks of diverse psychological and psychiatric problems. These things will happen specifically with the material abundance in the background, showing us that what we lack in our world is not material sustenance, but the *sensation* of living. This is how Kabbalah explains the process that lies ahead.

The way to meet this challenge is to utilize Kabbalah to understand the source of suffering. This will sweeten the suffering, since we will see that there is a reason for it. This will allow us to begin the correction *before* we plunge into affliction. This is why we are working so hard to prevent, rather than to cure, and prevention means letting humanity become aware of the wisdom of Kabbalah before it plummets into deep depression.

Perhaps it will be easier to come to terms with Kabbalah's concept and purpose of suffering if we understand its perspective on death in general. Here's what Kabbalah says about death: We are all individual parts of one spiritual *Kli*, called *Adam ha Rishon* (The First Man). The soul of *Adam ha Rishon* was split into billions of souls that came down to this world. This world occupies myriad bodies, each with its own soul. The goal is for each person to return to the same root in *Adam ha Rishon* from which he or she came down.

When we first come into this world, our souls are but a "point." If we do not build a spiritual *Kli* out of this point while living in this world, our souls return to their roots in *Adam ha Rishon* like seeds that did not evolve, unconscious, lifeless points. To put it differently, we do not feel our own existence until our souls dress a new body in this world.

However, if we cultivate this point through the altruistic intention until it becomes a spiritual *Kli*, that *Kli* will remain after the demise of our physical bodies, since we've begun to feel the Upper Force while living in this world. This connection remains, since it is not a part of our biological body.

The spiritual *Kli* perceives what is outside of us, regardless of our natural sensory perceptions. Once we are outside ourselves, physical life and death do not affect how the soul perceives. Therefore, we don't feel life and death in this world so intensely, since spiritual sensations remain intact. Put more accurately, eventually we must transcend this biological alternation between life and death to the point that we are not affected by it whatsoever.

# QUANTUM THEORY

The following is
Dr. Jeffrey Satinover's lecture
at an international Kabbalah congress,
Israel, April, 2005

This lecture will focus on a field that is considered to be "advanced science," but which, compared with Kabbalah, is actually quite primitive. Think of a person who doesn't know what a nut looks like, and suddenly finds a nutshell. He spends a long time studying it and for many years assumes that it is a completely lifeless object. Finally, after long, arduous years of research, he examines the complex symbols on the inner part of the shell and concludes that this has to be a shell of a living object, probably containing within it a living, evolving organism that is not the shell itself.

Just like that person, modern science has been successfully researching the physical world for hundreds of years, assuming that this world is the whole reality. The premise was that the physical world was a lifeless entity, and that there was nothing else besides it. Science has recently concluded that if we meticulously test the purely physical world, we will be able to find subtle evidence that the physical world is only a shell covering a living entity inside it.

Let me try and explain why specifically modern quantum theory is a kind of "boundary science." There is an extensive debate around quantum theory, so I will present only what I think is correct. I also recommend that you study this topic on your own to know what other researchers have found, and then draw your own conclusions.

I would like to stress that quantum mechanics and modern science do not say anything about Kabbalah or about spirituality.

However, they do say that the physical world is not the end. They have proved that there is something beyond, but they cannot say a thing about its nature. I think that accurately defining this point is of paramount importance.

All our knowledge, coupled with the immense power of quantum theory and its inferences about the physical world, lead us to deduce two things:

1. There must be something beyond the physical world.

2. We do not know anything about that "something" and cannot research it through science.

We often want science to serve as a tool in the research of spirituality. But the best scientists have already realized that this is not possible. Science can serve as an intellectual tool, leading us to conclude that there is something else. In Kabbalistic terms, it can be a vessel that leads us to knowing the point in the heart. The most abstruse mathematics in quantum mechanics can be a tool that enables us to recognize the existence of a point in the heart. But science cannot reach beyond that point.

\* \* \*

Let me try to give you a short, easy introduction to quantum theory. I will not use sophisticated mathematics and I will only present terms you have probably heard before. If these terms did not make sense before, I congratulate you, because they are not supposed to make sense.

Ancient Kabbalists said that it is impossible to imagine the true nature of reality. Contemporary quantum mechanics came to a very similar conclusion. It is impossible to use any terms or images to properly understand the nature of the physical reality. For instance, many of you must be aware of the famous statement that when you understand matter correctly, you understand that it is simultaneously a wave and a particle. This is a very trendy saying, and perhaps you are imagining something about it, or are setting up a little mental equation.

In fact, however, this is nothing but a line of utterly senseless symbols. There is no way to make them sound logical.

I previously stated that quantum theory allows us to understand the boundaries of contemporary science and declares that there is "something" beyond the physical world itself. To explain this, I will later describe an astounding phenomenon whose research is now evolving, called "quantum computation."

In addition, I will relate to a witty experiment that was first described conceptually back in the 1960's by Richard Feynman (1918-1988), one of the greatest physicists of the 20th century and a Nobel prize laureate in physics. This depiction is, even today, the most concise description of the mystery that surrounds quantum mechanics. Later, this experiment was executed with various kinds of particles. I will offer my explanation as to why this science demonstrates the boundaries of science, and why it points directly to the existence of "something" beyond the straightforward material world.

For generations, the fundamental perspective of science matched that of Einstein. Einstein's perception still prevails among many scientists, maintaining that there is nothing besides the physical world. Since the brain is built solely of physical particles, any specific event, meaning interaction of one particle with another, is defined wholly by the location of the particles and their movements in the preceding moment. The same perspective applies to every event in the physical world, including events in our bodies, our minds, our thoughts, and our interconnections.

In other words, the entire physical universe is a lifeless mechanical mechanism inevitably and inescapably unfolding. Any perception that we think is our own, the very perception of ourselves as conscious, feeling human beings, with our own intentions, (everything we do here and the rest of our human life) is only an illusion. There is no love, no hate, no passion, and no satisfaction. We are lifeless particles in complex compositions that unfold over time.

All our progress in medicine is founded wholly on that perspective and, thanks to it, succeeded. Many of us owe our lives to it. This perspective is a very compelling one and cannot easily be discarded.

Yet, this principle brutally attacks not only our perception of ourselves, but our need to ascribe purpose and meaning to life. Nonetheless, as exasperating as it may be, a large part of the world functions in just such a mechanistic manner.

Many contemporary philosophers recognized that while this view yielded great benefits, it inflicted an alarming blight upon us because of the belief that life is ultimately meaningless.

The Nazis, for example, readily applied this perspective in many fields and became very efficient as both killers and scientists. Often, modern medicine's attitude towards people is cold and cruel primarily because of the efficiency of the perspective that life has no meaning.

Computer science is a kind of extreme distillation of the mechanical outlook down to the mathematics and the logic of mechanical interactions. The scientific basis for modern computer science is the idea that a physical entity can exist in several states simultaneously. The computer consists of components that are based on "bits," and contains an enormous amount of them. A "bit" is a physical entity that can exist in one of two states.

Modern quantum mechanics allows for a phenomenon with far-reaching implications. It maintains that there can be physical entities that exist in two states simultaneously. Just believe me for a moment—such a thing really does exist. This means that if a standard computer can be in N states, a quantum computer can be in $2^n$ states at the same time.

At the Yale University laboratory, we have built a device that contains 400 such components. This may seem like a relatively small number, but such a device can produce a memory of $2^{400}$ bits. This is such a huge number that we cannot even perceive it. Thus, we are talking about building computers of such fantastic power that could literally work magic.

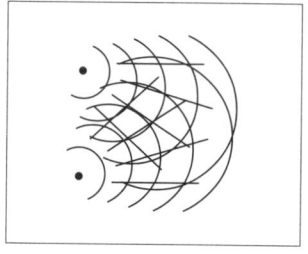

**Figure 8**

How did the assumption arise that two different states could exist simultaneously? Here we should mention an experiment conducted by Richard Feynman some fifty years ago. Assume that there is a full water tank containing a device that moves up and down. This action creates waves from two different sources, causing the waves to cross paths. Eventually, the path-crossing of the waves will create a pattern known as an "interference pattern" (Figure 8). This pattern is a collection of the path-crossing of the waves. It is a very well known phenomenon and we can easily calculate where these crossing points will be.

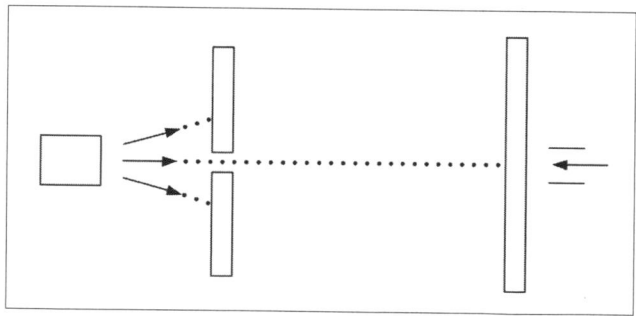

**Figure 9**

Now let us picture a similar experiment, but with particles instead of ripples. Picture a gun shooting discrete bullet-like particles at a screen. If we put a partition between the particle gun and the screen with a tiny crevice in it, and shoot particles toward the screen, only a thin ray of particles will penetrate the screen through the crevice. Consequently, the particles will always appear at a certain predictable point (Figure 9).

If we changed the experiment a little and made two slits in the partition instead of one, we would expect particles to reach two distinct points on the screen, just as we had one distinct point on the screen when there was only one slit. However, if we built the experiment correctly, at a certain ratio between the size of the particles and the size of the slits, the result would be quite different: We would find that the particles appeared all along the screen, not just in the two anticipated points.

As a result, particles would appear in even spaces along the whole screen and in both directions, indefinitely. The quantity of particles at each point would differ, being more profuse at the center and gradually decreasing as we move away from the center. The proportion between the number of particles appearing

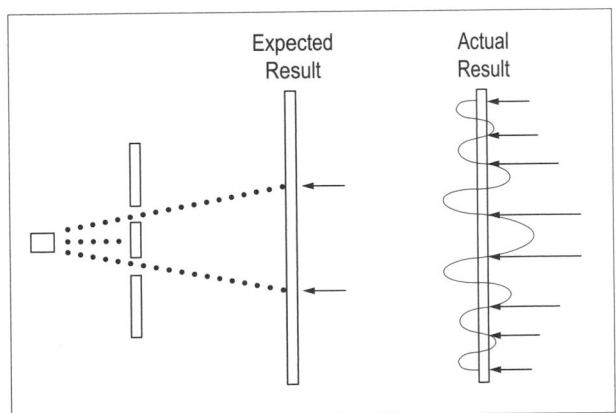

**Figure 10**

at each point would create a wave pattern (Figure 10). As a result, one could say that quantum particles are both waves and particles simultaneously.

This brings up the question, "What is a wave?" To simplify how this works, I will first explain it with limited accuracy, and subsequently correct the inaccuracy. A wave is a division of probabilities to find a particle at a certain point along the screen. Actually, the particle gun projects a "moving wave of probabilities," a probability that a certain particle will be at a certain location.

Now let me correct myself: When we measure the numbers that describe the amount of particles that appeared at each point on the screen, we get a mathematical result that does not perfectly match a moving wave of probabilities. Instead, it is the square root of the probability.

In fact, some of the square roots are negative. The probability that something will happen in the real world can be anywhere between 0 and 1, but it cannot be negative. In other words, this "thing" that expands in space doesn't exist in the physical world, but it still creates an impact.

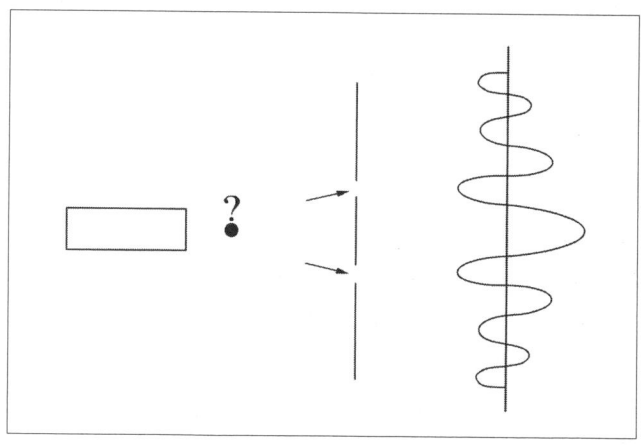

**Figure 11**

Even if we were to fire one particle per week, the probability distribution would remain identical to the interference pattern of the two waves we mentioned above. Actually, even if we fired a single particle, dismantled the equipment, put it back together a year later, and fired another single particle, we would still receive exactly the same result (Figure 11).

This probability pattern is built with absolute mechanical precision. It is so astounding that it seems to reach beyond time and space. The structure of this phenomenon is prearranged in perfect mechanism, its mathematics are known with utter precision, and today this phenomenon assists us in building amazingly accurate computation devices.

If we were to fire a single particle, we would be able to predict with utter mathematical precision the probability of that particle hitting a certain spot on the screen. However, quantum mechanics says, and this is my main point, that nothing in the physical universe can determine *exactly* where that particle will hit.

In other words, when you are looking at millions of particles, matters are determined with absolute mathematical certainty. However, the specific location where each particle will land remains undefined by anything in the physical universe.

As a result, some of the greatest physicists deduced that there was a deterministic element in the universe that operates precisely as we've thought. However, there is another unknown operative element delicately interwoven in the texture of the universe that does not interfere with the mechanical unfolding. This is why it all appears mechanical in the eyes of one who is not observing sufficiently keenly.

However, if we observe very cautiously, we will find that any particular unfolding in the universe is affected by something that is *not* a part of the universe. Moreover, since the theory itself requires an element that is essentially extra-universal, we are left with a boundary.

This is why some physicists proclaimed that quantum physics was a boundary science, a science that points to the boundary which humans can reach while researching the physical universe. In other words, these physicists assert there is something beyond that boundary that science will never be able to identify.

# THE CREDIBILITY
# OF QUANTUM THEORY

Any theory can be proven wrong. Quantum theory, too, is only a theory and may turn out to be mistaken. Moreover, even today there are scientists who consider it erroneous and are searching for alternatives.

In the world of science, it is common for one theory to fall and for another to rise in its place. However, there is a subtle distinction to be made here. Let me explain by comparing the Newtonian theory with Einstein's theory of relativity. First, let's assume that there is a stick that is moving in space. According to Einstein, if we make the stick move extremely fast, it will begin to shrink. According to Newton, regardless of the velocity, the stick will remain as it is. Thus, we have two competing theories.

Some will say that Newton's theory is completely false and that Einstein's is correct. Indeed, if we look at the question superficially, this will be a true statement. However, the fact of the matter is that this statement is false.

The precise way to decide between the two theories is to say that Newton's theory is a boundary case of Einstein's theory. This means that in most familiar circumstances, sticks cannot move nearly as fast as it takes for us to see them shrink. Therefore, in most cases, Newton's explanation holds true.

However, Einstein's perception is generally correct. Not only is it true regarding familiar velocities, but it would also be true if we were to accelerate the speed to such a high velocity that we could actually see the stick shrinking.

If science discovers a new theory that says today's depiction of reality by quantum mechanics is a boundary case, then everything we have said about quantum theory will remain true. If you state that it is incorrect, then you will have to show that it is totally and essentially false. Such a possibility always exists, theoretically, but quantum mechanics has thus far proven itself as the must successful scientific theory in the history of science, passing more rigorous tests than any other theory to date. Hence, it is highly unlikely that it will be essentially refuted.

* * *

At its origin, science was based upon a religious worldview, perceiving the world as a living entity where diverse spiritual forces operated, such as ghosts and demons. Later on came modern mechanical science that determined that the previous theory was a complete fallacy, and that the world could best be understood by using the mechanical principles of physics and chemistry.

Mechanical science determined that there were no ghosts or demons that dwelled in, and operated, matter. Instead, it postulated that matter is operated by cause and effect. Chemical reactions do not happen according to the phantoms of alchemy, but according to quantifiable chemical reactions that can be mechanically controlled by mathematics.

This mechanical approach made possible our huge progress in understanding matter and its modus operandi. It also led to numerous technological innovations that have benefited us for many years. As we said earlier, modern medicine is fundamentally established upon this mechanical worldview.

Until the 1930's, the predominant belief was that biology was different from all other sciences. It was believed that although a living organism was made of chemicals, it was nonetheless operated by a living entity that was not mere matter.

However, the evolution of contemporary biology could take place only after it was decided to discard the idea of the living entity. Professors that insisted on supporting the old concept were discharged from universities. Thus, modern genetic engineering, molecular biology, and pharmacology progressed through the lifeless mechanistic approach of reducing living bio-systems to nothing more than complex machines.

There is a very interesting point concerning the connection between physics and other sciences: All the sciences—chemistry, biology, zoology, anthropology, sociology, and every other science—designed their models according to the mechanistic perception of the crown science—physics. Actually, this process continues today.

In many universities the world over, various sciences have yet to adapt their models to the 19th century models of physics. The problem is that physics has already abandoned these models. Even molecular biology, which studies the most minuscule objects, has yet to turn to the path that the quantum revolution has paved.

About a year ago, I gave a course at the department of biochemistry in the University of Toulouse, France. The head of the department was unaware of the fact that to understand the evolutionary process of protein, one needed to take quantum effects into consideration, and that this is why it cannot be understood in terms of classical mechanics. This is just an example of how even "fundamental" sciences such as biochemistry have not internalized the implications of quantum mechanics.

Even in its home court, in physics, most physicists have not yet grappled with the implications of the discovery that events unfold in the physical universe without being completely determined by prior events in the physical universe. This concept is still shocking to the prevailing scientific perception throughout the world.

We are in the midst of a slowly progressing conceptual revolution. More and more physicists, biophysicists, and biomolecular scientists are beginning to understand the impact of quantum mechanics. However, only a handful has recognized that evolution incorporates quantum effects in the design process of organisms. When these scientists began to face this conceptual revolution, some of them grasped the far-reaching implication—that the mechanistic view was outdated, and that something else had come to replace it.

On a personal note, I'd like to say that even as a young man, I felt that the mysteries of the physical world hid a deeper mystery. Even before I knew what quantum physics was about, I assumed that plunging into its depths would lead me to the spiritual world. In addition, I was always intuitively drawn to Kabbalah. Whenever I came across it in its genuine form, I felt that it manifested an inherent truth.

# The Essence
## of the
# Wisdom of Kabbalah

# STRIVING FOR BALANCE

As children, many of us believed that the world was filled with all kinds of forces, like ghosts in fairytales. As we grew, we gradually relinquished this belief, but every now and again we still feel as though these forces actually exist.

The truth of the matter is that we are searching for them every single moment. We want to know about the world we live in because if we do not, we will never be freed of the sensation of uncertainty, to live in peace and confidence. We are curious to understand the world we live in and to improve our state of being. This curiosity evokes questions such as, "Who am I?" "Where am I?" "What shall become of me?" Such questions prompt us to strive to know the reality in which we live.

Reality is divided into two parts: the human being and his or her surroundings. Some claim that we should only study and change ourselves, asserting that by so doing, we will feel tranquil and regard the world more positively. Others, however, say that we should stay as we are, make the most of what the world brings to our doorsteps, and change the world to fit our needs. Either way, it does not seem that our lives are working very well.

The best state in which we can get along with the world is that of equilibrium. If everyone understood me and wanted exactly what I want, that would be a state of equilibrium. There is no state more perfect than the sense of being in balance with the world. It can only be compared to being a fetus in my mother's womb: everything exists only to care for me; there is no need to erect any defenses.

Science refers to that state as "homeostasis." The Greek word, *homo,* means *same* or *similar*, and *stasis* **is** Greek for *condition*. This is the state of being that every object in reality strives to achieve.

The laws of physics, chemistry, and biology explain that the only reason for any movement of matter, whether still, vegetative, animate, or speaking, is its longing to be in balance with its surroundings. For us, as human beings, to be in balance with our surroundings, we must know about the nature of the surrounding world and how we can equalize with it.

Only then will we know how to arrive at a state where everyone wants what we want, think the same thoughts, and hold no grudges against others. Thus, everything would unfold in peace and love. This is the goal for which Kabbalah exists; it teaches us how to obtain peace among all humanity, and between humanity and nature.

All of our inquiries of the world and of ourselves are carried out by science. Regrettably, progress in science and technology has not made us happier. For all our efforts to arrive at a state of tranquility, wholeness, and happiness, our reality is growing harsher and more threatening each passing day.

But if we are all striving for the best, why are there problems? Problems exist because we do not know the general reality, how it behaves, its structure, or how it acts upon us. We do not know with what we must equalize.

It seems that as deep as we probe into matter, and as much as we try to understand our own nature and the nature of the outside world, we still fail to see what nature wants of us, why it exists, and the purpose of each element in nature.

Some researchers probe the outer layer of matter; others research deep into its structure, down to the molecular level and to the relationships between atoms and subatomic particles. The most advanced researchers claim that at a certain level, matter becomes elusive. From that point on, they do not understand what happens. However, the reason they are failing to understand existence below the subatomic level is not the lack of more sophisticated research tools, but the inability of human beings to fully perceive reality.

While we rely solely on our five senses, we feel that we can do with reality as we please. Once we enter the spiritual world, however, we realize that it is, in fact, reality that does with us as it pleases. From a certain level of spirituality and above, we understand that we are the ones who are building our own reality. In other words, we recognize that reality is a kind of projection of our own selves.

This last level is what contemporary researchers describe. They maintain that there is a certain limit beyond which we cannot perceive. This point between the perceptible, physical world and what lies beyond our perception is the meeting point between science and Kabbalah.

Kabbalah explains that there is a mode of research that allows us to penetrate the "level of causes." Using it, one can understand with certainty why the world exists, what it wants of us, and how we can exist in balance with it, a balance we will experience as peace and tranquility. Those who have already researched that realm are called "Kabbalists," and their writings describe the outcome of their research.

Kabbalists say that beyond visible matter stand Nature's will and deliberation, which surround the whole reality. This will and deliberation circumscribe reality, watch over it, and operate it in order to benefit it. Moreover, these will and deliberation constitute the general law of reality. In other words, the general law of reality is absolute giving, and all matter in reality must equalize with that.

The wisdom of Kabbalah helps us perceive the actual attitude of Nature toward us and feel it. In this way, we can treat Nature with the same attitude and thus equalize with it.

The levels of revealing the actual reality are called "worlds." Just as scientists delve into the structure of materials with microscopes, or probe into deep space with telescopes, so Kabbalists penetrate the thought that surrounds reality using the wisdom of Kabbalah.

Our progress in researching reality is a real adventure. We can begin to feel our past and future, and discover that time does not actually exist; that, in fact, everything already exists. A Kabbalist can move in time, as we perceive it now, and progress or regress beyond the present state.

People who can perform such "time leaps" are called "prophets." They do not envision or imagine the future, but simply move several degrees forward to a specific level of reality that the rest of humanity will someday reach. They speak to us "from there" and tell us what they feel in their "present time." They could just as easily be great historians, regressing to states that humanity once experienced, relive them, and tell us about them.

We can often find Kabbalistic writings that depict events before their own time, such as Abraham wandering from one place to another, meeting people, learning what he said and what he did. To know all that, a Kabbalistic researcher must turn back in time to reach the same state that Abraham did, meaning a specific degree, and tell us about that reality by being fully present in it. A Kabbalist can gather impressions from that time and convey them to us.

Baal HaSulam describes it in the following manner: *But, because those that reached the degree where Abraham stood, or anyone, they see and know what Abraham saw and knew. For this reason they know what Abraham would say, and likewise in all the sayings of our sages when they interpreted the verses of the Torah. All that was because they too attained the degree, and each degree in spirituality is a reality. Everyone sees the reality, as all those who come to the city of London in England see what is in the city and what is said in the city.*

–Baal HaSulam, *Shamati*, article 98
*Spirituality Is That Which Will Never Be Lost.*

In addition to the ability to move in time, Kabbalists discover other forces in reality. It is no coincidence that the legends speak of ghosts, demons, and angels. Even though they actually have a very different meaning from what we presently ascribe them, such forces do exist. A Kabbalist who researches the depths of nature begins to see its operating forces, connects to them, and uses them to benefit both self and all of humanity.

Admission to the study of reality does require certain efforts, but it also captivates one's whole inner life and provides complete fulfillment. A person who studies reality discovers the reason for our existence, knows where we all have to reach, and understands the reasons for our manifold problems.

Hence, Kabbalah is not mere theoretical scientific research. Rather, it is a practical method intended to help us through every moment of our lives. Through Kabbalah, one discovers the future, the past, one's attributes when he or she first descended into this world many lifetimes ago, and the way one still needs to traverse.

Seeing both ends of the rope, one understands what to do and how best to do it. Kabbalists can also see the forces operating on them at any given moment in time, such as why one should marry a specific individual, or why one's children are the way they are. All these details are predetermined. Today, in fact, even science acknowledges that this information is determined in the genes.

There is a famous story about twins who were separated at a very young age and lost contact with each other. Thirty years later they reunited and discovered that both had the same occupation, their wives had the same name, they had given their children the same names, and they even lived in houses with the same street number. Matters unfold this way because our internal information defines everything that will happen to us in each of the states we will experience in life.

Kabbalah names these internal prearrangements that guide one's course in life, *Reshimot*. The *Reshimot* exist in every person, and every state that one experiences is intended to teach something that will promote one toward obtaining the ultimate goal.

If we knew the forces that operated on us and our interior structure, we could prepare for every future state. If we knew how to be in balance with the general law of reality, reality would seem totally opposite from its present appearance.

The wisdom of Kabbalah is not meant to teach us about reality in a merely scientific manner so that we can philosophize about the "residents" of the Upper Worlds. Rather, it teaches us how to control our destiny every single moment. All of the forces and events that pressure us are intended to help us become leaders of our own reality. "Leaders of reality" means that we are in balance with reality at every moment of existence. Hence, our task is to discover what "being in a balanced state" implies.

## CONTROLLING THE MATERIAL WORLD

Kabbalistic researchers of reality discovered that reality consists of our world and higher worlds. The lowest of all worlds is our material world; the rest are all spiritual worlds. In the spiritual worlds, there is no such thing as physical matter in the form that exists in our material world. The substance of the spiritual worlds contains only desires, forces, and thoughts.

We think we can control the matter of our world, but when we rise to a higher level, we immediately realize that matter is but a consequence. Matter is operated upon By the Upper Forces, the Upper Worlds. Because we are not yet in those worlds, we are unable to control it.

If we want to change anything at all, we must rise to the degree above our own, where preparations were made before they were implanted in us. Only at that level will we acquire a certain level of understanding and ability to change anything at all. Life repeatedly proves that we do not control anything, and more often than not, we are in our golden years before we realize that life has simply flown by.

Notwithstanding technological progress, humanity is completely bewildered concerning its further progress. We are in a terrible state because we are as far as can be from balance, and until we acquire knowledge and strength to change anything at a higher degree than matter, we will not have a moment's rest. Only when we rise to the degrees and forces that operate our world will we reach the much-wanted balance.

## OPENING OUR EYES

All of reality is a single, unchanging thought of bestowal and giving. Kabbalists refer to this thought by the name, "The Thought of Creation." They say that its essence is the Creator's will to be good to His creations. If we do not relate similarly to that encompassing thought of reality, we are imbalanced with it, which we experience as suffering.

Of course, we do not naturally feel it. And even after we do, we find it hard to understand. But if we saw that this was how reality operates, we would change our ways.

Thus, our only goal should be to open our eyes and see that such is indeed the case. The wisdom of Kabbalah helps us to see it; when we do, we most certainly change.

If I saw that something could improve my situation, I would pursue it in any way possible. And if I had to give something to induce improvement, I would give it, as long as it improved my state of being. The primary difficulty is, therefore, to open our eyes and see what is presently hidden from us.

All our evolutionary states are preordained in the Thought of Creation, but the way and the pace at which we traverse them depend entirely on us. Indeed, we can tread the whole trail even today, and equalize with the Thought of Creation.

# THE STRUCTURE OF REALITY

Throughout its existence, humanity has been utilizing its five senses to research the reality in which it lives, and gather the findings to formulate sciences. The purpose of science and the accumulated human knowledge is to improve our lives and help us more effectively use the world we live in.

The wisdom of Kabbalah, unlike all other sciences, researches a realm whose existence eludes an ordinary person. To research this realm, one must be equipped with another sense, a sense that perceives the "Upper World." With this additional sensory ability, one can gather information about the Upper World and experiment with it. Like any ordinary scientist, a Kabbalist can record reactions to actions. Kabbalists are researchers of the Upper World, and as such, they have recorded their findings over thousands of years of research. The collection of their records constitutes the wisdom of Kabbalah.

The wisdom of Kabbalah describes the actions that originate in the Creator and hang down to our world through all the Upper Worlds. It also describes how they expand through the corporeal reality that we can all perceive with our five ordinary senses.

Our world is a consequence of the Upper Worlds. Thus, the wisdom of Kabbalah contains knowledge about the Upper Worlds and our world. The Upper Worlds pertain to a higher level of existence than our world, where time, space, and motion do not exist, but only abstract forces. It follows that Kabbalah contains the existence of all times as they are expressed in our world.

Kabbalah is a means to help us research all the states of existence. This sequence of states includes our state before our souls dress in physical bodies, all our phases while we exist in this world, and our situation once the soul departs from the body and returns to its root in the Upper World.

Kabbalah deals with everything that expands from the Creator to the reality that He has created, and which He leads to His desired goal. Kabbalah does not deal with the Creator Himself.

In light of the crisis that humanity is facing and the growing sensation of helplessness and emptiness, the time has come for the wisdom of Kabbalah to appear. Kabbalah explains that the purpose of reality is to raise humankind to a level of equality with the Creator. The purpose of humanity's decline to this world is to enable us to rise independently to the highest level in reality—the Creator's level.

While in this world and ascending towards the Creator, we hold both ends of reality, as we are in our world physically, and in our souls at the level of the Creator. This is the purpose of our existence, predetermined by the Creator Who leads all of us toward it.

At the end of all our physical incarnations in this world, our souls will reach the degree of the Creator. This process is similar to any other gradual process in reality. From the Creator's point of view, the beginning of the process and its end are at the same point. But while there is no concept of time for the Creator, for us the process extends over millennia, a long enough period for us to acquire the necessary insights and qualities to evolve. These will help us gradually become more Creator-like, and to ultimately become equal partners with the Creator.

The process is essentially one of gradual evolvement. The evolutionary process of humanity is like the ripening of a fruit: dry and sour while unripe, and sweet and juicy at the end. Had we not known how fruits ripen, we would have erroneously thought that the sour fruit would ripen to an even more sour fruit. But since we know the good end of the process to begin with, we can justify the whole process. Thus, only those who know the end of the process can justify it; if we, too, could see our future state, we would understand the Creator's actions and justify them.

## ON THE LADDER OF DEGREES

"Climbing the degrees of the Upper Worlds" is a generic term for all the new discernments collected along the spiritual way, the perpetual internal improvement, and the new qualities that one assumes at every moment.

As previously mentioned, the creature consists of a will to receive pleasure. This will is divided into five elementary parts, called "five degrees of *Aviut* (thickness)." They are graded from *Aviut* zero (root) to *Aviut* four. Thus, the term *Aviut* serves to measure the intensity of the desire.

Each of the basic degrees of *Aviut* is divided into five subdegrees, and each of those is divided once more into sub-subdivisions. Thus, the will to receive is divided into 125 degrees, and we are required to correct all of them.

Correction of the desire means using the desire for pleasure to bring pleasure to another. Such a use is called "giving" or "bestowal." The attribute of the Creator is bestowal, and the abundance that expands from Him to His creatures is an expression of His desire to give to them.

Hence, correcting the human ego from wanting to please self to wanting to bestow is considered an ascent in degrees. With each degree, one acquires more of the will to bestow, and accordingly feels more like the Creator. With each ascent, one comes closer still to the attribute of the Creator and to the purpose of life. The process persists until one acquires the attribute of the Creator to the fullest and becomes identical to Him.

To allow human beings to correct, the Creator created the worlds and their degrees *before* He created humans. Only afterwards was humankind created and lowered to this world. From here we humans must climb back to our roots. Consequently, Kabbalah deals with two successions: "from Above downward," pertaining to the cascading of the worlds and their degrees, and "from below Upward," pertaining to the soul's ascent through the very same degrees.

The worlds that stem from the Creator are *Ein Sof, Adam Kadmon, Atzilut, Beria, Yetzira, Assiya,* and finally, our world (Figure 12). Kabbalah describes both the creation of the worlds and how a soul descends from the Creator through all the worlds down to ours. Between the Upper Worlds and our world is "the barrier" that separates the material world from the spiritual world.

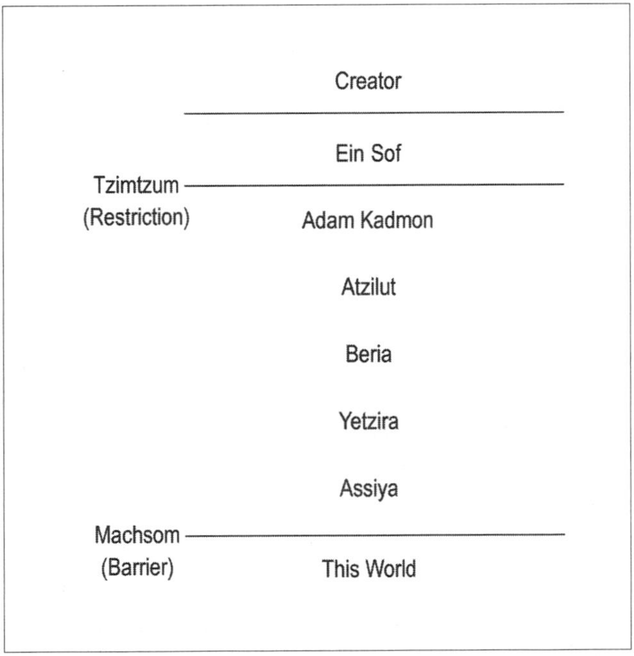

|  | Creator |
| --- | --- |
|  | Ein Sof |
| Tzimtzum (Restriction) | Adam Kadmon |
|  | Atzilut |
|  | Beria |
|  | Yetzira |
|  | Assiya |
| Machsom (Barrier) | This World |

**Figure 12**

Below the barrier, the body and the soul are at the level of this world, and we begin our correction process at this level. From this world, the soul ascends by accumulating knowledge of the spiritual reality, traversing the worlds *Assiya, Beria, Yetzira, Atzilut,*

*Adam Kadmon*, ultimately returning to the world *Ein Sof*. There, in a state called *Gmar Tikkun* (The End of Correction), the soul is completely reunited with the Creator.

The wisdom of Kabbalah encompasses the entire reality below the Creator: the worlds, everything within them, the descent of the soul to this world, and its return upwards. In other words, the wisdom of Kabbalah contains all of humanity's states and situations.

All the worlds, including ours, stand one below the other. Hence, all the worlds comprise the same elements. The Light emerges from the Creator and traverses all the worlds down to this world. Therefore, each element that is present in the world *Ein Sof*, is also present in all the other worlds. Kabbalists define this relation as "root and branch":

*Thus, there is not an item of reality, or an occurrence of reality found in a lower world that you will not find its likeness in the world above it, as identical as two drops in a pond, and they are called "Root and Branch." That means that that item found in the lower world is deemed a branch of its pattern found in the higher world, being the root of the lower item, as this is where that item in the lower world was imprinted and made to be.*

—Baal HaSulam
*The Essence of the Wisdom of Kabbalah*

We therefore see that every element and detail in this world, with all its connections, is present also in all the Upper Worlds, from *Assiya* to *Ein Sof*. The universe, Planet Earth, the still, vegetative, animate, and the speaking are all found in the worlds above this world, too. There is only one difference between the elements of this world and the elements of the Upper World: in the Upper Worlds the elements are forces, and in our world they are matter.

Attaining the Upper Worlds enables one to see the forces that operate upon every item in this world. When we attain the Upper World, we come to know the modes of behavior of every element of that world's reality, the reason for its behavior and its qualities. The wisdom of Kabbalah facilitates our ascension to the Upper World and permits one to observe every object's behavior in this world from above.

Crossing the barrier is a gradual process. Studying Kabbalah with the goal of nearing the Creator's attribute—the attribute of bestowal—enhances one's keenness. Increasingly subtler insights surface, pertaining to the reality in which one lives. One begins to feel the operations at the "backstage" of matter, the forces that operate the visible, perceptible matter.

A Kabbalist continues to feel the same reality as before with the ordinary five senses, but at the same time perceives the forces beyond the perceptual boundaries of the five senses with the help of the sixth sense. The hidden reality becomes more and more lucid, and the existence of another reality beyond the picture of this world becomes apparent.

The revelation of the spiritual reality is divided into three phases, called *Ibur* (gestation), *Katnut* (infancy), and *Gadlut* (adulthood). In the first phase, the *Ibur*, we can see our state, but cannot understand it. In the second phase, the *Katnut*, we understands that something is happening, but still cannot independently participate in spiritual action. In the third phase, the *Gadlut*, we obtain the strength and wisdom to participate in spiritual action and affect the spiritual reality.

At the third level, we begin to determine the flow of forces from the Upper World to our world and back. As individuals, we then become active participants, conduits through which the flow travels from above downward and from below upward. At the level of *Gadlut*, we realize our part and operate as a connector between the worlds. This is our corrected state, and each person must reach it.

Each person can come to feel every item and element of every world. All that we need is a special, subtle sense, an ability to discern and to feel. Even in this world, we discern considerable differences between the sensations of a young child, a youth, an adult, and a scientist. The study of Kabbalah continually builds new insights and discernments in us, eventually leading to the perception of the Upper Worlds.

From the above we can understand why Kabbalah contains all the teachings and sciences of this world. Without proper explanations, we would be lost and think that Kabbalah is a mystical teaching of wizardry and miracles.

There are others who relate it to Judaism, but in truth the wisdom of Kabbalah has no connection whatsoever with mysticism, religion or any other manmade fantasy. The purpose of the wisdom of Kabbalah is one: to bring humanity to congruence with the Creator through gradual correction.

Kabbalah is such a successful method for the correction of humankind's egoism precisely because it is written by those who are corrected. One's desire to draw near to the states described in Kabbalah books makes those states "project a correcting force" upon one's present state. This force is called "Surrounding Light." It changes one's qualities, enabling individuals to sense their corrected state by gradually forming altruistic qualities in them.

The study of Kabbalah focuses on the world *Atzilut*. The world *Atzilut*, called "The World of Correction," is above the *Parsa*. It is a system designed especially to correct a person whenever one wishes it. The Light that fills the corrected soul of a person in the world *Atzilut* shines upon one's present state as Surrounding Light, a force that corrects human nature from egoism to altruism. The Surrounding Light elevates the soul through all the worlds until it returns to its root. Thus, the world *Ein Sof* is the ultimate goal, our world is the starting point, and the improvement of human attributes is called "ascent in the degrees of the worlds."

Kabbalah is for those who ask about the purpose of their lives, those who are not satisfied with mundane pleasures such as sex, wealth, honor, or knowledge. When the whole of humanity awakens to ask about the purpose of life, the wisdom of Kabbalah will emerge. Kabbalists pointed to the year 1995 as the beginning of this time, hence the necessity to disseminate it.

## FOUR LANGUAGES IN THE WISDOM OF TRUTH

Kabbalists, as previously mentioned, research the Upper World, the world beyond the perception of an ordinary person. Hence, the depictions of Kabbalists' attainments relate to the Upper World, but because we are not aware of the existence of a spiritual world besides our own, we ascribe their words to our world, a phenomenon called "materialization."

When the Torah (Five Books of Moses) was written, the people of Israel were at a spiritual degree. But after two thousand years of detachment from spirituality since the ruin of the Second Temple, the Torah stories seem to refer to historic episodes or moral conduct.

Yet, this is not the case. Each element in the world is connected to the same element in all the other worlds by a "root and branch" connection. Based on that principle, Kabbalists developed a language that relies on the parallelism between the Upper Worlds and our own world. In it, processes unfolding in the spiritual world are described using names of branches taken from our world.

Kabbalists use four different languages to explain how we can reach the degree of the Creator and how we can draw to ourselves the Correcting Force that will invert our nature from egoism to altruism. These languages are the language of the Bible, the language of laws, the language of legends, and the language of Kabbalah.

In his essay, *The Wisdom of Kabbalah and its Essence,* Baal HaSulam wrote that there are four languages in the wisdom of truth, and the essence of the wisdom of Kabbalah is no different than the essence of the Bible. However, the laws, the legends, and the language of Kabbalah are the most convenient and appropriate to use.

The difference among the languages is in their accuracy. The language of Kabbalah is more precise in depicting the connection between the root in the Upper World and the branch in the lower world. The more accurately one connects oneself to one's Upper Root, the greater Correcting Force one receives.

The language of Kabbalah applies to terms that do not exist in our world, such as "worlds" and "*Sefirot,*" charts and formulae. This language makes it easier to avoid confusion and materialization, and facilitates a clear and ordered approach to the study. The language of Kabbalah is essentially different from other languages because of the clear, unequivocal way it describes the purpose of Creation—the similarity of the creature to the Creator, i.e. inversion of egoism into altruism.

The chief Kabbalah textbook at present is Baal HaSulam's six-volume *Talmud Eser Sefirot (The Study of the Ten Sefirot),* based on the writings of the Ari. In just over 2,000 pages, *Talmud Eser Sefirot* expounds on the structure of the Upper Worlds, accompanied by charts, glossaries, and tables of questions and answers for revision of the material. In the introduction to the book, Baal HaSulam elaborates on the reasons for preferring the language of Kabbalah to the other languages in our generation.

Today, humanity has come to the last phase in the evolution of the will to receive. This is why Baal HaSulam adapted the method of the Ari to the structure of the souls in our generation- -to make it accessible for everyone.

## CHANGING MYSELF

Many people mistakenly relate the wisdom of Kabbalah to the Jewish religion. In truth, Kabbalah and religion are fundamentally different. The purpose of religion is to calm people down; it nurtures the hope that if I pray, the Creator's attitude toward me will change.

Kabbalah takes a very different approach: The root of the word "prayer" (Hebrew: *Tefila*) means "sentencing," or "judging" (Hebrew: *Palal*). In other words, one sentences oneself, examines the difference in quality between oneself and the Creator, and asks to receive strength to correct one's own attributes.

The wisdom of Kabbalah explains that the Creator is unchanging. His attitude toward His creatures is categorical—He is good and does good to both the good and the bad.

Everyone feels the constant pressure of the Upper Force according to his or her distance from It. When one is far from the Upper Force, the pressure is heavy, and when one comes nearer to the Upper Force, the pressure eases.

Although the Upper Force engages diverse means to draw us near It, Its purpose is always the same—to bring every human being to perfection. If we want a change for the better, it is we who must change. We have to rise to a higher level, and in each ascent we will feel ourselves closer to the Creator and our souls will be fulfilled and satisfied. There is no other way to induce change in our lives.

All through history, humankind has been begging for a change that would come from the Upper Force, but change has not come. The Upper Force waits for the change to come from us.

Until we evolve through the wisdom of Kabbalah, our paths will remain filled with affliction. Blows that push from behind compel us to find another place that seems better. But it only takes a while for us to see that the new place is not as good as it first seemed. Thus, we relocate and the scene repeats itself.

However, if we evolve through Kabbalah, our corrected state will project to the present state and illuminate it. With this Light, we will know how to move forward. If we know the correct goal to begin with, we will be drawn to it gladly. This is the difference between ordinary human evolution and evolution according to the wisdom of Kabbalah.

Today, the world is evolving unconsciously, without understanding the reasons for its existence. Humanity does not know where it is being led and why every person is born, lives, and dies. The wisdom of Kabbalah opens our eyes and guides us to the perfection and eternity that come with obtaining the Creator's degree.

When we begin to examine our position in reality using the wisdom of Kabbalah, we find that the Creator's attitude toward us is purposeful. It becomes evident that asking the Creator to change *His* attitude is pointless. If we move forward with the help of the Light, our pace will exceed the sufferings and we will progress ever faster. This is the whole benefit from the study of Kabbalah: accelerating spiritual progress to beat suffering.

Today, at the beginning of the 21$^{st}$ century, humanity is at the brink of a chasm: drug abuse is escalating, and despair and the fear of total destruction will not leave humankind a choice but to flee the suffering that will goad us from behind.

From all the above, we can clearly see that discovering that the Creator's attitude toward us is purposeful is of paramount importance. This attitude of the Creator enables us to turn to Him as to a fellow traveler and ask Him for the help, wisdom, and strength to progress toward Him. Such a request is answered by the Creator instantaneously. He will disclose the Upper Worlds, and teach us how to progress.

Just as we teach our children to use their surrounding reality wisely, so does the Creator teaches Kabbalists. He reveals to them the spiritual worlds and admits them within these worlds. In this state, Kabbalists feel the Forces that operate in reality and begin to independently and wisely participate in the process.

The wisdom of Kabbalah shifts one from progressing through the negative force that pushes from behind, to easy and rapid progress through the Positive Force that pulls from ahead. Kabbalah is unique in that it develops our ability to recognize evil and acknowledge it. It develops subtle, keen insights of good and bad.

The difficulty in discerning good from evil is that the real evil—our ego—seems good to us. We are accustomed to treating our egos as a means to evolve. In fact, our pleasures, our livelihoods, our very essence and our personal selves are felt in our egos.

Kabbalah helps to discern what causes harm, how it can be mended, and allows us to progress in each phase of the evolution. The difference between a highly evolved individual and a less evolved one lies in the ability to discern good from bad.

We can compare this to a gauge. The smaller the unit the gauge measures, the higher the precision of the instrument. The study of Kabbalah makes us increasingly sensitive to the discernment between spirituality and corporeality, between bestowal and self-reception.

If a contemporary person has the opportunity to hear about Kabbalah and the possibilities it offers, such a person can realize his or her purpose of creation: to rise through all the worlds up to *Ein Sof* while living in this physical world.

## THE RIGHT ATTITUDE TOWARDS REALITY

Kabbalah in Hebrew means "reception." As its name testifies, Kabbalah teaches how to receive. With the right attitude towards reality, it is possible to experience endless enjoyment. This endless enjoyment is not from sex, food, a new car, a big house, or other transient, mundane pleasures. Instead, it is from those delights that can fill us with such utter bliss that we would transcend any sensation of time to receive them.

We sense the passing of time by the fluctuations between good and bad feelings, or sensations of fulfillment and absence of fulfillment. However, when we are in a state of elation, we are unaware of time. The wisdom of Kabbalah tells us that we can eliminate time altogether, along with the sensation of distance and any other limits or boundaries. One who has reached such a state is clearly living in an infinite, unlimited world.

Our lives will always contain two opposing elements—pleasure and desire, plus and minus. A pleasure that pervades a desire satiates it and cancels it. We come across this phenomenon in every area of life. When the plus neutralizes the minus, we end up feeling nothing at all. As long as we short-circuit pleasure and desire, we will be locked in a zero-sum equation. However, put a resistor between these opposites and they will work perfectly, creating everlasting enjoyment.

Kabbalists explain that pleasure stems from the Upper Force. This Force sends us pleasure because It loves us. When we try to receive the pleasure directly, the pleasure cancels our desire to enjoy it and the pleasure stops.

Yet, there is another way to relate to the pleasure: If we could discover the love of the Upper Force towards us and return His love with ours, we would become equal to the Upper Force. Each party would want to please the other, and the desire to please the other would be each party's enjoyment. Thus, the pleasure would be

coming from without, originating from within each party, a consequence of each party's love for the other. This is why pleasure from
love does not quench the desire for it, and the creature receives an
endless sensation of pleasure, which is felt as endless life.

Let us clarify this with an example: When a mother gives her
daughter a candy, the daughter enjoys the pleasure of the candy's
flavor. As soon as the candy is finished, the pleasure fades. However, if the daughter related to her mother, instead of to the candy
itself, she could think of her mother's love for her, which is why she
gave her the candy. She could then decide to receive the candy
not because it was tasty and pleasing, but because she wanted to
return her mother's love.

The way she could express love for her mother would be to
receive the candy that her mother wanted to give her. Thus, the
daughter would not relate to the pleasure from the candy, but
to the joy that her mother received from her daughter's pleasure
from the candy.

This creates a completely new relationship between the giver
and the receiver. Now, the two have equalized. Thus, the problem of the plus and minus that neutralize each other is solved
because the receiver—a minus—has become a giver—a plus. If the
vessel receives the Light solely to return the Upper One's love, it
completely equalizes with the Giver, the Upper One. The pleasure
no longer extinguishes the desire, and the pleasure lasts.

It is of no importance who gives and who receives. Only
the *intention* matters, the way by which we relate to giving and to
receiving. We can relate to the Upper Force in such a way that we
will not be receivers from It, but Givers of It. Such an intention
would enable us to receive not because we want the pleasure, but
because we want to please the Upper Force.

At the end of the process, and because we act as the Upper
Force does, we will gradually acquire Its reason, stature, and de-

gree. When we can execute this process within us, we will begin to feel a connection with the Upper Force; we will feel that we have acquired Its reason, that we are learning how to receive from It and how we can give It pleasure. It only takes this simple act of changing the intention to become increasingly similar to the eternal, boundless Upper Force.

To perform such an act, we need the disclosure of the Upper Force, the sensation that there is an Upper Force, that It loves us and wants to fill us abundantly. If we felt all that, we would begin to sense the relationship between ourselves and the Upper Force. Thus, the only difficulty before us is finding a way to discover the Upper Force, feel It and maintain contact with It.

The study of Kabbalah helps every person develop this kind of contact. This relationship between a human being and the Upper Force begins once a person feels there is a "field" that sustains the whole reality, an Upper Force, and that he or she is inside It. If we only begin to feel that this Force exists and that It relates to us lovingly, wanting us to know and come closer to It, we will naturally begin to develop this kind of relationship.

People who experienced clinical death speak of a sublime Light that awaits us, and many scientists are also beginning to consider similar concepts. But it is not necessary to experience such predicaments to feel this Light. The study of Kabbalah can gradually enable us to sense the Upper Force. We begin to research reality and operate according to what we discover and perceive.

When we feel this Force outside us, we discover that the Upper Force loves us; we then begin to feel that the Upper Force exists to benefit us and that It wants us to enjoy. We develop our reciprocal attitudes accordingly.

There is no fantasy here; these are very real and measurable things. Kabbalists measure the shape and power by which this Force comes to them, the pressure It puts on them, the corresponding resistance they have to apply, how they can connect to It, resemble It, in which of their desires they can already be like It, and in which they still cannot.

Kabbalists are impressed by the Upper Force and return its love to the extent that the Upper Force appears to them as loving, as wanting to benefit them.

We are "vessels that feel," hence everything begins from our sensation of the Upper Force. We all want something. If we could feel that this something came from someone, our attitude to reality would change drastically; now, we would have someone to relate to. The study of Kabbalah can help us feel the Upper Force, the sensation of the Giver.

## THE OUTSIDE REALITY

The minute we begin to feel the Upper Force and build a relationship with It, we begin to feel the outside reality. Kabbalists say that there is nothing around us but the Upper Force, that we are in a field that fills the whole reality. When we begin to feel this field, our bodies become completely insignificant. We begin to feel where we exist permanently, endlessly, with or without our bodies. In such a state, we no longer depend on the sensations we receive through our five senses.

We begin to perceive the external reality beyond the five senses in addition to our natural sensory perception. When that happens, physical life or death no longer matters. This state is above the sensation of life we experience while we are in our "box"; we become connected to the boundless stream of life surrounding us. Although we do continue to exist in this world, we simultaneously live in all the worlds, forever.

Such a sensation is evoked by perceiving the two forms of reality: the reality perceived in our five senses, and the outside reality. As a matter of fact, the sensation of the outside reality overshadows the sensation of the reality perceived in our five senses because it is far more intense, boundless, and unlimited.

## CROSSING THE BARRIER

When the Upper Force appears to a person as loving and evokes the Form of bestowal in that person, one "crosses the barrier" and enters "the spiritual world." This process is very similar to the way photographs were developed. When I was a child, we would take pictures on a film and dip the film in chemicals to develop the pictures. When the film was immersed in the chemicals we would watch how the picture gradually became clearer.

We are used to treating the world as a reality where people, organizations, and public institutions influence the course of our lives, such as our neighbors, our employers, and our government. Slowly and gradually, through actions aimed at discovering the Upper Force, we will begin to feel what truly stands behind everything that happens in the world. We will begin to see how this Force operates people like puppets on strings, and we will understand what It wants of us.

Slowly, through our life experiences, we will begin to see that everything comes from a single attitude of someone, this Upper Force that operates on us. This is the point from which the wisdom of Kabbalah truly begins.

Everything that happens prior to this is called "the preparatory period," before the crossing of the barrier. From the moment one begins to feel the Upper Force and comes in contact with it, one begins to understand the instructions in the Kabbalah books that are written especially for the reader. These books tell Kabbalists what they should mind, what to do, and which reactions they can expect.

This process is similar to the way grownups teach children to behave. Because children do not know the rules of conduct in this world, we warn them of things that might fail them and suggest how they should behave. Kabbalists have written their instructions for us in precisely the same manner. Books of Kabbalah are actually manuals that inform us how we can advance more quickly and improve our relationship with the Upper Force, a relationship we call "the spiritual world."

## EQUIVALENCE OF FORM

We have thus far established that the nature of the Light is opposite from that of the vessel: one is giving and the other receiving. When Light fills the vessel, it cancels it. In other words, the desire to enjoy is neutralized by the pleasure that satisfies it. As a result, people are engaged in a constant pursuit of new pleasures, but never manage to hold on to them. No real pleasure is possible as long as the contact between the Light and the individual is based on the individual being a receiver.

To receive real pleasure, one must receive with the intention of pleasing the Upper Force. If one maintains that intention, he or she will be fulfilled and will always be a giver. The profit from such reception is twofold: one is filled with both the pleasure and the recognition of the Giver. If one receives in order to please the Upper Force, one begins to know the Upper Force, which in turn brings the receiving person a sensation of the outside reality.

If we receive from a solely egoistic interest, we only feel ourselves. Receiving with the intention of giving to the Upper Force enables us to know the Upper Force. Through such a reception we transcend our own "box" and experience our surrounding reality.

The sensation of the outside reality brings us to a level of existence that supersedes the existence of life and death in this world. Reception by egoistic interest, called "corporeal reception," is disqualified, and the person transcends to reception in the soul, called "reception in order to bestow" upon the Upper Force.

For one to begin to receive in order to bestow, one must feel the Upper Force. The sensation of the Upper Force as a Giver evokes shame in the receiver, resulting in that person's decision to receive only on condition that he or she can return pleasure to the Giver.

Yet, the Upper Force is hidden in our world. Were it disclosed, we would all enjoy a twofold egoistic pleasure, from the pleasure and from the contact with the Upper One. Such a state would egoistically "lock" us on the Upper Force extracting pleasure from It, and we would never be able to switch to returning love to the Giver.

Thus, the first condition for the sensation of the Upper Force is to be rid of egoism. The sensation of the existence of the Upper Force cannot be perceived in the human ego. If we had perceived the Upper Force with our egoistic desire, we would become a *Klipa* (shell). A *Klipa* is such an intense egoistic desire that one is unable to break free. The only way to be rid of the ego is to equalize in form with that of the Collective Soul.

## THE COLLECTIVE SOUL

We are all created as one *Kli* (vessel) called *Adam ha Rishon* (The First Man). We are tied together in that *Kli* as parts of a single system. To enable the *Kli* to correct, the spiritual structure of *Adam ha Rishon* was shattered into numerous particles. These particles are the individual souls that clothe our bodies in this world. The result of the shattering is that each person is confined to his or her egoistic desire, oblivious to others and feeling only oneself.

Today, after a long evolutionary period, people are beginning to feel the points in their hearts, the points that drive them to reconnect with the Upper Force, to search for spirituality. At this stage, we must obtain the strength to overcome our egoism and transcend it, since we will be able to connect to the Upper Force and draw near it only to the extent that we equalize with It.

The way for us to connect with the Upper Force is for those who share the same spiritual goal to join together. Although each of them is subjugated to their individual will to receive, they all wish to transcend it. Such a social environment is defined as a "spiritual environment." With it, one can break the wall that separates him or her from others.

While those in a "spiritual environment" may still be egoists, they are nonetheless doing their best to create a structure similar to the corrected structure of the soul of *Adam ha Rishon*. We cannot succeed in this task alone, as such a task contradicts human nature. What we can do is acquire an intense desire and join with others.

This is where the wisdom of Kabbalah comes in. Books on Kabbalah describe the corrected state of the souls and the difference between these and corrupted states. The key difference is the intention with which we use our nature. Correction means that we change the purpose for which we use our desire—from inducing self-gratification to benefiting others.

When we correctly study genuine Kabbalah, we come to depict our own corrected state. This depiction prompts the Light that already fills our corrected state to correct our soul. Once that Light corrects our soul, It fills it, and we begin to experience the spiritual world.

* * *

There is no time in the spiritual world, no space, and no motion. The Upper Worlds are not above us in the physical sense of the word. "Ascent" actually means "regaining consciousness."

The study of Kabbalah requires us to shed our corporeal clothes of familiar mundane sensations and perceptions, and penetrate through matter and into the Forces behind it.

In spirituality, we turn from observing the picture of reality to knowing the Forces that paint it. We begin to understand how reality is made, acquire the ability to connect to the Forces that created the picture and ultimately govern them. Kabbalah is our key to the "Control Room" of reality.

# Perception
## of
## Reality

# BUILDING THE SPIRITUAL *KLI* (VESSEL/TOOL)

## MAKING THE *KLI*

The gist of our work is the making of the *Kli*. If we know how to build our tool of perception correctly, we will understand where we truly are. As we have said in the previous section of this book, our substance consists of a desire to receive delight and pleasure.

If we can make this substance sensitive to insights concerning reception and bestowal, we will be able to use it to perceive the spiritual world. It is similar to the way a block of crude iron is melted to create engine parts. When assembled correctly, they yield a working engine.

Similarly, we must work with ourselves to perceive spirituality. Building the spiritual *Kli* is a lot like sculpting—you must carve the raw material and file it until the desired shape appears. The raw material, in this case, consists of our desires, our thoughts, and intentions.

The Creator formed Creation with the intention of doing good to His creatures. To realize His goal, He created a *Kli*—a will to receive—that would receive His benefit. At first, this will is shapeless. Shaping the will to receive is the work of us all until it is robed in its final form—bestowal, the form of the Creator.

The substance itself remains as it was first made—a will to receive pleasure—but changing the intention to bestowal likens its modus operandi to that of the Creator. Thus, the intention *is* the form.

Kabbalah books depict the forms that one should create in the will to receive, degree-by-degree, to finally sense the benefits that come from the Creator. The general will to receive consists of 613 desires, and each of these is topped either by an aim to receive, or an aim to give. These forms of reception or bestowal that "cover" each desire determine one's degree of spiritual attainment.

A degree is a certain level of strength of the Form of bestowal. This enables the benefits of the Creator to manifest within the will to receive. The diverse fillings within the will to receive are the origin of the many names of the Creator. It is the perceiving individual who names the Creator according to the flavors he or she feels within the Creator's bestowal.

Once the Kabbalists attained the nature of reality and studied it, they divided the manner of recognition of reality into four levels: Matter, Form in Matter, Abstract Form, and Essence. Kabbalah is a practical study method that leads researchers thoroughly and systematically along the evolutionary trail. As in any other scientific method, Kabbalah teaches the researcher what to do, which results are to be expected, and expounds on the reasons for them. Kabbalah *does not* engage in depicting theoretical states that one cannot carry out independently and with full awareness.

Kabbalah defines the boundaries within which reality can be correctly perceived: Matter and Form in Matter. Kabbalists perceive the additional discernments, the Abstract Form and Essence, only vaguely and without certainty; hence Kabbalah does not engage in these forms at all.

These boundaries apply to research in both corporeal and spiritual worlds, as the soul perceives the spiritual world exactly as it perceives the physical world. Even in our world, responsible researchers and scientists do not study Abstract Forms or Essence, but explore only Matter and Form in Matter.

## THE REACTION OF THE SENSES

We exist in the world, but we do not know what is outside of us. For example, we do not know what exists outside our ears, we cannot identify the "something" that pressures our eardrum. All we feel is our own reaction to that "something."

Hence, the name we give an exterior phenomenon is actually the name of our own reaction to it. Quite possibly, there are different frequencies or phenomena from those that we create inside our ears. However, our ears react in a unique manner to the unknown "something" on the outside, and it is that reaction by which we define that phenomenon. All we can do is study our own reactions to phenomena, meaning what happens inside of us.

It follows that our perception of the world is very limited. If we begin to understand that what we see is not what is actually happening outside of us, we can approach the research on how we perceive reality in a whole new way. In fact, there is a certain Essence that operates upon us, but we will never feel it in its true form. All we can feel is our interior reaction to it. Our picture of the world is the sum of our interior reactions, but we have no way of knowing what is actually present outside of us.

If we want to relate to reality correctly, we must acknowledge the limits of our perception. We cannot delude ourselves into thinking that we perceive the real picture, as we have no true perception of its Essence or Abstract Form. We can only recognize the Form that dresses in our own Matter. Although it is regrettable that we must limit ourselves, it is nonetheless the way things are.

As we have said, we cannot perceive the full picture, only our reaction to it. We also cannot know just how close our perceived Form in our Matter is to the Abstract Form that exists outside our Matter, and affects it.

In the same way we feel our surroundings, the spiritual *Kli* perceives the spiritual reality. This *Kli* can feel only its own reaction to the Light within it; it cannot say anything about the Light outside of the *Kli* that perceives it.

It is through its intrinsic reaction that the *Kli* understands and determines what is Light, what is a *Kli*, what the Light wants of the *Kli*, and what the *Kli* wants of the Light. All of these depictions have no connection at all to the phenomenon as it is outside the *Kli*.

Baal HaSulam was very insistent on explaining these matters in his *Preface to the Book of Zohar*, since Kabbalah deals solely with building a *Kli* for the perception of reality:

*For example, the sense of sight offers us only shadows of the visible essence, according to how they are formed opposite the Light. Similarly, the sense of hearing is but a force of striking of some essence on the air. The air is rejected because of its force, strikes the drum in our ear, and we hear that there is some essence in our proximity.*

*The sense of smell is but air that comes out of the essence, strikes out nerves of scent, and we smell. Also, the sense of taste is but a result of the touching of some essence on our nerves of taste.*

*Thus, all that these four senses offer us are but manifestations of the operations that stem from some essence, and nothing of the essence itself.*

*Even the sense of touch, the strongest of the senses, separating hot from cold, and solid from soft, all these are but manifestations of operations within the essence; they are but incidents of the essence. The hot can be chilled, the cold can be heated; the solid can be turned to liquid through chemical operations, and the liquid made into air, meaning only gas, where any discernment in our five senses has been expired. Yet, the essence still exists, because you can once more turn the air into liquid, and the liquid into solid.*

*Thus, you evidently see that the five senses do not reveal to us any essence at all, but only incidents and manifestations of operations of the essence.*

~Rabbi Yehuda Ashlag (Baal HaSulam)
*Preface to the Book of Zohar*, item 12

Thus, proper perception of reality is of paramount importance to us. The boundaries are not set to limit or diminish our knowledge or to stop us from engaging in some forbidden matters. On the contrary, when we detach ourselves from the parts we do not control, we spare ourselves confusion. If we limit our field of vision to the range we can control, we will perceive the true picture of reality. Following this condition rigorously will enable us to progress correctly.

In our present state, we have no perception of the Upper Light at all. This is so because of the oppositeness between our egoistic vessels and the altruistic Light. If our vessels were to match the Light, meaning if we were to match the desire to receive and the Light, we would be able to perceive it. Such "matchmaking" is called "clothing." Clothing pertains to attaining the intention to bestow over the desire to receive, an intention that one can receive only from the Light.

To receive that intention from the Light, one must have "a point in the heart," or a fragment of Light within the will to receive. Using this, one can begin to nurture one's matching between one's *Kli* and the Light. The point in the heart is a fragment of intention to bestow, and with it one can begin to use the rest of "the heart," meaning the rest of the will to receive. If one can use one's desire with the intention to bestow, this will be considered "clothing the Light."

Let us return for a minute to the way our sense of hearing functions: To hear, we must always maintain equilibrium of pressures between ourselves and our surroundings. To balance the pressure on our eardrum from without, a delicate mechanism creates equal pressure in the opposite direction from within. Hence, we seemingly measure the pressure from the outside, but in fact, we measure the pressure we create within, in response to the pressure from without.

All our measurement tools work according to this principle. We can demonstrate it using a mechanical weight. Several objects participate in this measurement: a spring, a dial, and the object about to be weighed. Placing the object on the device creates a downward pressure (Figure 13). To balance the pressure, the spring pulls upward. The dial then measures the upward pressure the spring is applying, and presents it as the weight of the object. Measuring the pressure of our internal mechanism is defined as "measuring Form in Matter and Matter."

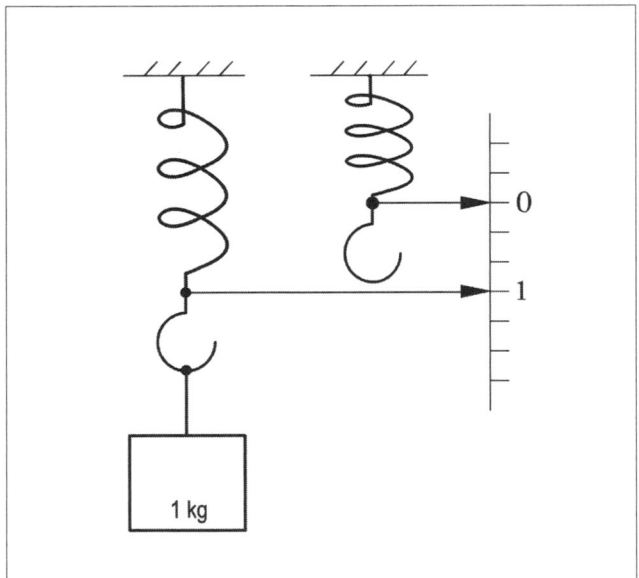

**Figure 13**

Now let us return to the spiritual *Kli*. Form in Matter, in spirituality, is the reaction of the *Kli* to what is outside of it. It is called "intention." The intention with which the substance (will to receive) is used balances what comes from Above, i.e. from the Creator. With it, a Kabbalist can measure the similarity of intention to the Creator's intention toward him or her.

A Kabbalist perceives the full scope of the will to receive delight and pleasure. If the Kabbalist can use part of it with the intention to bestow, this would be a spiritual act. This is because using any part of the will to receive with the intention to bestow means he or she has thus balanced the Creator's pressure. Such an act is called "building a spiritual *Partzuf* "(face), a term that indicates a measure of equivalence between the Creator and the creature, between the Light and the *Kli*.

Kabbalists use *Partzufim* (plural for *Partzuf*) to test how much the Creator wants to give and how much pleasure they can give back to the Creator. For example, if the strength of the intention to bestow that one can work with clothes twenty percent of the Light, the remaining eighty percent of the Light will be rejected without receiving them. In other words, one can only balance with the Creator in twenty percent of one's will to receive, one's substance. This is why that person will not activate the remaining eighty percent of the will to receive, and will restrict them.

Our perception of the Creator depends on the power of our intention over our Matter. Just like the weight and the spring, we cannot measure anything but our own intention. The intention to bestow is the Form that we measure, hence the term, "Formative Learning," that Kabbalists use to describe how we learn.

We often called the intention to bestow "a sixth sense." This term emphasizes that with the intention to bestow, one can feel what is present beyond one's five natural senses.

Our sixth sense works just as our five senses do. The only difference between them is that the five original senses are naturally present in us, while the sixth sense is one that we must build by ourselves. While the sensitivity of the natural senses may vary with age or other elements, it is generally true that it is natural for us to have five properly working senses.

As previously stated, it is we who must build the sixth sense. This is because the sixth sense is not a sense in the usual meaning of the word, but is rather an intention. Our task is to study the forms by which the Creator bestows, and when we do so independently, we build ourselves as "creatures" that exist in our own right. This is the difference between humankind and all other parts of Creation.

## BUILDING THE RIGHT FORMS

The spiritual world is hidden from us. Hence, we cannot understand how to attune our tools of perception correctly; we simply do not know what it is we must perceive. For this reason Kabbalists come to our aid and advise as to how we should position our tools of perception so we can perceive the Upper Light.

Kabbalists say that the Upper Light is abstract. However, that does not mean that any form that human beings might create will enable them to perceive anything of the Upper Light. Perception of the Upper Light is possible only when one adjusts one's *Kli* to one of the 125 Forms intended for just that purpose.

Thus, the spiritual ladder consists of 125 degrees. Each degree designates a more advanced form of receiving Light in one's *Kli*. Kabbalists describe how we can locate these forms, study them, and apply them to our Matter. They also teach us how to design our will to receive in such a way that we can "present ourselves" before the Upper Light in forms that are "suitable" for the Light.

There is a similar phenomenon that manifests itself on the corporeal level. Many researchers claim that humankind cannot perceive an external phenomenon as long as it is not present in a similar form in that person's mind.

The film, *What the Bleep Do We Know?*, offers a good example of that concept with a story about the Native Americans who watched Columbus' armada arrive at the shores of America. The story has it that the Indians standing at the seashore couldn't actually see the ships that anchored not far from land. The shaman, an imaginative man, was troubled by the unusual movement of the ripples without any apparent reason. For many hours he gazed at the water trying to figure out what was causing the ripples.

Through his efforts, he finally managed to discern the shape of the body that produced the ripples and thus was able to see the ships. Subsequently, he described what he saw to his tribesmen, and because they trusted him, they, too, succeeded in creating the form of the ships, until they all saw Columbus' ships.

Kabbalah asserts that nothing exists outside the human mind. Creating the model of the ship in the shaman's mind built the picture of the ship for him, which the shaman thought existed outside of him. Actually, a ship does not exist on the outside whatsoever; it is only we who are conditioned to relate to reality as independently existing in an outside reality in which we are making daily discoveries. Kabbalists, however, say that all innovations are merely new models inside our own minds.

Once we acquire a true vision of reality, we feel that the previous vision was completely fictitious, like a dream. If we want to perceive the actual reality, we must build real models within us. This is the meaning of the ascent from the fictitious world to the real world. Indeed, this is why humankind was given the wisdom of Kabbalah, and what evokes these models within us.

# PERCEPTION PATTERNS

Our tools of perception can never perceive the Essence, regardless of our degree. Although what we perceive is indeed the Essence, we can only perceive it through Matter, and we cannot even imagine what the Essence itself is like. Moreover, we cannot even *want* to perceive the Essence.

For example, none of us feels that an additional sixth finger would be welcome. However, if we could imagine that we once had a sixth finger, and that we could do something with it that we cannot do today, then we could talk about a need for a sixth finger. But if we never had an additional finger, we could not even imagine how it would benefit us. This is why we will never want a sixth finger.

Similarly, since we never felt an Essence, we cannot want to perceive the Essence. Attainment of Matter, the manifestation of the actions of the Essence that is present within the Matter, is quite satisfactory.

The above discussion raises an important question: If we cannot perceive the Essence, how did Kabbalists know that it exists? For the time being, we will leave this question unanswered, but we promise to return to it later.

\* \* \*

The will to receive is the Matter. It is divided into five degrees. When the will to receive is integrated with the intention to bestow, it adopts different Forms, from the most opposite from the Creator to the Form of the Creator Himself. While spiritually evolving, we gradually study all the qualities that Matter might assume. This is called "Formative Learning."

We have a genuine desire to acquire the Forms of bestowal that are dressed in Matter. A genuine desire means that it is a desire that stems from having had this Form before and not having it now.

Our Matter, the will to receive, was first created in a corrected Form, meaning the Form of bestowal, which was then inverted to reception. Reacquiring the Form of bestowal through our own efforts is the essence of our correction. This process should be carried out using the same pattern that was created while we had the Form of bestowal, and is based entirely on practical experimentation. Hence, this process is entirely reliable.

Philosophy, however, engages in ideals abstracted from Matter. It is completely opposite to the method of Kabbalah because it is founded on the study of Abstract Forms. Philosophy discusses qualities such as truth, falsehood, anger, and valor while not clothed in Matter, ascribing Abstract Forms titles such as "truth is good, lying is bad." This creates a concern that people will relate to such declarations as ideals and will adhere to them fanatically.

Baal HaSulam demonstrates this with a parable about a person with such high regard for the quality of truth that, when faced with an opportunity to save people from death, he chose not to because it involved telling a lie.

This parable demonstrates the mistake of engaging in Abstract Forms because we have no means to judge a certain quality as good or bad when it is not clothed in Matter. Only when the Form is clothed in Matter can we determine if it is beneficial to the evolving of Matter or detrimental to it. The only criterion is the evolution of Matter toward realization of the purpose of Creation.

\* \* \*

While we could erroneously imagine Abstract Forms, the Essence is something completely unimaginable for us. We logically assume that behind the Form that dresses Matter and the Abstract Form, there is a foundation that sustains all other Forms, which we call "Essence."

Thus, we see that our ability is limited, that we can only attain Matter and the Form clothed in it. Yet, we cannot avoid asking why the Creator did not create us with the ability to perceive the Abstract Form and Essence.

The answer to that is simple: If we could attain the Abstract Form and the Essence, we would see the Essence clothed in everything, operating everything, from the very first to the very last state. Such a clear picture would rob us of the sensation of freedom of choice; it would prevent us from studying the image of the Creator and building It within us.

Having shown that nothing exists outside one's *Kli*, we can now define the terms "this world" and "Upper World," as depictions of the modes of perception of reality. "This world" is the perception of reality within the *Kli* while we are working in order to receive. The "Upper World" is the perception of reality within the *Kli* while we are working in order to bestow, altruistically.

## THE FULL PICTURE

Kabbalists describe only what they attain with certainty within their vessels, meaning the Form in Matter and Matter. Matter is the will to receive and the Form in Matter is the Form of bestowal dressed within the will to receive. In fact, the creature always attains the full picture, but the question is, how certain can we be of what is disclosed?

For example, when we perceive a certain picture, how do we know what we are perceiving? Which part of our perception of the picture is certain and which is not? Since our tools are limited we cannot be sure. Perhaps the spectacles through which we are observing reality are showing a plain ahead of us when, in fact, there is a chasm right before our feet. Could our next step throw us into the abyss?

If the above example seems unlikely, the next will clarify matters: without radiation gauges, how would we able to detect radiation? We could easily walk into contaminated areas unknowingly.

We are unable to build tools to assist us in determining the trustworthy from the untrustworthy in spirituality. The difference between what we can or cannot rely on lies in the difference between the various tools at our disposal.

Attainment of Abstract Form and the Essence are not considered certain attainment. This is because they are perceived through "external vessels," not through "internal vessels," although we do sense in them something called "a remote luminescence." Such luminescence induces a sensation that something exists, but it is not clearly perceived by the senses. This is the answer to the question of how Kabbalists know about the existence of Abstract Form and Essence.

\* \* \*

We should stress that locating the gateway from this world to the spiritual world is not a direct action. It is more like a search for an exit from a closed circle. Although the opening is in a certain place, it can only be seen after having searched all 360 degrees.

To build the Form of the Creator within, we must first know all the Forms opposite from Him. If the Creator had an image outside of us, we would be able to adopt it immediately and thus end the process. However, such an image does not exist outside of us; it is for us to build the image of the Creator within our own Matter. First we must learn about the opposite Forms to the Creator, and only then can we build similar Forms to Him. The sum of the images creates our image of the Creator.

## CREATING MODELS

Let us briefly return to Columbus' ships. The shaman could not detect the ships because he didn't have the model of such a big "floating house" in his mind. In Kabbalistic terms, we would say that he didn't have the *Kli* to detect this Form. For the shaman to detect the ship, its form would have to preexist in his mind, which he would compare to the observed form. He would then recognize it as a ship on the basis of equivalence of form between the preexisting model and the ship he saw on the outside.

However, to be able to feel the spiritual reality, we must come across someone who would tell us about it. Hence, Kabbalists write their books. We can use these books to depict what is outside of us and gradually build the spiritual Forms or patterns within us.

The patterns we would build within would unquestionably be false, but the very effort and the craving would make the Light affect us. The Light builds increasingly similar shapes to its own shape until one begins to see the actual Light. This is the only way to advance, since only the Light can build the vessels within us. In truth, we cannot imagine what is actually happening around us even now. We are surrounded by worlds and powers that we cannot sense for lack of equivalence of Form.

## A CAVEMAN IN TODAY'S WORLD

If we think some more about the Indians and Columbus' ships we might ask this: If a caveman were to be born in today's world, would he see the cars and the buildings? The answer is that he would not. Would he then bump into buildings or be hit by a car as soon as he left the sidewalk?

Before we answer these questions, we must understand that we perceive only such Forms that our senses are equipped to detect. For example, the air around us, which seems empty, might actually be as condensed and solid as cement. We are accustomed to seeing this world as a space where we can move about freely. But if we build appropriate tools of perception, we will feel that the world is actually filled with the Creator's enormous powers, which do not allow us any free movement. If this were to happen, we would feel totally controlled by the Creator, as if we were "planted" in cement, unable to make even a single free gesture.

Because our caveman would not have the sense that perceives the wall as Matter or as Form in Matter, he would be able to go through walls as if they were air. Kabbalists wish to direct our observations so we can perceive the world correctly. If we were to draw ourselves just a bit off our ordinary perception of the world and into the real perception that Kabbalists describe, this world may seem very strange to us.

Today, many quantum physicists are discovering that the world has a "strange" regularity of time, space, and motion. For example, they say that objects can be in more than one place at a time. This oddity leads them to think that everything is measured with respect to the observer. This means that the existence or absence of the caveman's wall, as well as the ability to move through it, are measured solely by the state of the perceiver's vessels.

We are born into this world with five tools of perception—the five natural senses—and these senses evolve from generation to generation. The environment surrounds every newborn child. As a result, when we grow we perceive the things around us as solid facts, as Forms in Matter perceived by our five senses.

Yet, even our perception through the five senses reflects what our own senses project, nothing more. I am the creator of the buildings, the cars, Earth, the universe, and my whole reality. I create them in my vessels, in my sensations. Outside of me, they are amorphous.

It is very hard to detach ourselves from our natural perceptions. It seems that a different outlook on reality is possible only
after we cross the barrier to the spiritual world. Only then do we
understand that things might be different than they first seemed.

For example, we cannot go through walls because we are
controlled by the very same rules that we create. But the Upper
Light is abstract; it is we who limit It. There is only one law in
reality: "the law of equivalence of Form." The more we equalize
our own form with the Light's, the more liberated and unlimited
we become.

Our will to receive is divided into 613 desires. According to
our difference in Form from that of the Light, we erect boundaries around each and every desire. The sum of all these limits
creates the shape of our internal tool of perception, and that tool
produces our depiction of reality.

It will be easier for us to understand the law of equivalence
of Form if we consider how radio receivers work. A receiver can
pick up waves only when it creates identical waves within it. Similarly, we "pick up" things that seemingly exist on the outside—but
only according to what we have created within.

The law of equivalence of Form is constant and circum-
scribes the whole reality. It is valid for both altruistic and egoistic
vessels. In other words, we perceive the corporeal reality and the
spiritual reality in exactly the same way—through equivalence of
Form. The only difference between the two kinds of vessels is in
their directions: one is aimed toward the self, the other toward
the Creator. However, existence in egoistic vessels permits a very
limited number of vessels to be felt.

Quantum physicists are beginning to discover that beyond
a certain boundary of research, the world seems to "vanish."
Kabbalists wrote about such "discoveries" thousands of years
ago. They explained that beyond this boundary, the physical

matter and its shapes disappear, and only forces and shapes that are above Matter remain. Continuing to study from this boundary onward will be possible only after researchers acquire the appropriate altruistic vessels.

Kabbalists depict the ground rules for the appropriate attitude to reality with much greater depth than scientists ever will. Only once these rules have been applied will it be possible to progress in the research and perception of reality.

Kabbalah was kept hidden until recently because humanity was not ready to understand it correctly. The achievements of contemporary science have prepared us to understand the wisdom of Kabbalah. This is why Kabbalah is being disclosed today.

Let us return for a minute to the caveman who stumbled into our time. We tend to think that our vessels are richer than his because we can see Forms that for him are nonexistent.

However, this is a mistake: while we have indeed evolved and acquired impressions of more Forms than did the caveman, building many more vessels, these vessels actually limit us more. Forms in Matter that we perceive were Abstract Forms for the caveman; they did not exist for him, and hence, did not limit him.

In the future, we will discover that the more we "acquire," the more we limit ourselves. We progress by acquiring forms and building more and more structures, but in the end these structures limit us on every level of reality and show us that we are not at all free.

As we evolve, we absorb numerous impressions from our environment: our parents, teachers, friends, and experiences. These impressions make us look at reality according to our inner "self-programming." Thus, reality is only a projection of our interior software; it does not exist outside our internal vessels. Reality is a figment of our imagination, but our minds portray its image as existing on the outside.

As with the physical reality, the spiritual reality does not exist outside us, but is really a Light dressed in a *Kli*. Outside the *Kli* is only abstract, shapeless Light, and all we are really talking about is applying Forms to the will to receive.

Kabbalists state that in the spiritual reality, the will to receive can adopt a finite number of discrete Forms. By joining all these Forms, we can perceive that of the continuous influence of the Light, which is the very image of the Creator.

Corporeality is a replica, a projection of spirituality, like an offshoot of a root. Hence, the process that unfolds in corporeality is very similar to the spiritual process. The egoistic will to receive can assume a limited number of Forms, after which matter disappears—similar to what researchers are discovering today.

After one builds a great many Forms, these become a single picture of "one" bestowal or "one" reception. This is a projection of the spiritual state called *Gmar Tikkun* (End of Correction). *Gmar Tikkun* is a spiritual state that happens after the *Kli* has robed itself with all the Forms of bestowal of the Light. In such a state, the Light and the *Kli* equalize completely.

The only way by which the vessel can accelerate constructing the Forms it currently lacks is by choosing the appropriate environment for spiritual progress. Such an environment would make one "imagine" the Forms described in Kabbalah books, and thus induce the action of the Light upon one's soul. The Light, in turn, will then build "sensors" to detect Forms of bestowal.

In fact, this Light is the same Abstract Form into which everything "disappears," as quantum physics has discovered. This Abstract Form projects the Form of bestowal upon the will to receive, and as a result, the "sensors" to perceive It begin to formulate within us.

Kabbalists define this Light as "the Light that reforms" because it creates the Form of bestowal within us, and thus brings us closer to our perfect state.

Today, many researchers believe that at the most fundamental level, we are all one, and that the connection between us should be one of love. However, these researchers will not find a way to realize this ideal because the Force to make this correction must be drawn from "the other side," the side of love. This can only be done through the study of Kabbalah.

Eventually, researchers will discover that matter vanishes entirely and that the only thing that exists is pure thought, but they will not be able to progress beyond that. They will sense that there is another existence beyond our own, where our Matter is opposite to our present Matter, and that we are connected in perfect unity. Yet, the way to obtain that Form of existence, the realm at the "other side" of quantum laws, can only be taught by those who are already "there"—Kabbalists.

It is impossible to break that barrier without drawing the Light found in Kabbalah books, because these are the only texts that were written from the "other side." One's desire to "get there" along with the study of the right Kabbalistic texts draws Light upon that person and builds within that person's soul the Forms in which one perceives the spiritual realm. Just like the shaman had to build the right shapes to see the ships, we have to build Forms of bestowal to be in the spiritual realm.

# REGAINING CONSCIOUSNESS

## US AND THE WORLD

From birth, we have the tools to perceive the physical reality. Within these tools are "information bits" about the states and shapes that we are destined to realize—the *Reshimot*. Through education and environmental influence our tools evolve until we have "normal" perception of the physical reality.

However, this is not the case concerning the perception of the spiritual reality. We have no "standard" by which to test if we are building our inner vessels correctly to disclose the attribute of bestowal and the discovery of the spiritual reality.

We do not know what to do with our desires, how we should shape them, and with which intentions we should prepare them. To assist us in this task, Kabbalists provide us with the necessary definitions. They teach us how we can calibrate our tools of perception to perceive the spiritual reality.

We perceive the physical reality in a predetermined manner; we were born and raised without being asked our opinions in the matter. The physical perception patterns that were formed in us while maturing make us sense the Light of *Ein Sof*. This Light actually stands opposite us all the time—the physical reality within which we and the world around us exist.

Yet, nothing is preordained as far as the spiritual reality is concerned. We must find our own ways of perceiving spirituality, and only the tools that we will build will provide each of us understanding about the Creator, the Upper Force that builds and influences everything.

We should keep in mind that reality is built within us. Our inner qualities reflect a "shadow" upon the abstract Light, thus creating our world pictures, the spiritual as well as the physical.

Thus, the way we will perceive the Creator depends solely on our own qualities.

* * *

The wisdom of Kabbalah has maintained its stance concerning the perception of reality for thousands of years. Conversely, science cultivated its approach through several key stages.

The classic perception, whose protagonist was Isaac Newton, states that the world exists in and of itself, regardless of whether or not we are there to perceive it. As the science of biology evolved, it enabled us to see the world through the eyes of other creatures. We discovered that different animals perceive the world in very different ways.

For example, a bee sees tens of thousands of pictures, which combine to create the picture of the world around it. A dog perceives the world primarily as "spots of scent." Then, Einstein discovered that changing the observer's velocity produced a fundamentally different picture of reality.

These discoveries opened up a second approach that asserted that the picture of the world depended on its perceiver. Perceivers with different qualities and senses perceived a different picture of the world. Thus, as in the first approach, the world still existed independent of its perceivers. The difference between the first and second approach is that the world appears different in the eyes of different perceivers.

A third approach that evolved suggested that the observer affects the world, and thus affects the picture that the observer perceives. According to the third school, the perception of reality is like an average picture between the attributes of the observer and the attributes of the observed object.

In other words, the observer perceives something in a certain way because this is how the observer is built, compared to the actual quality of the world. This approach asserts that there is a correlation between the individual and the world in the sense that the perceiver influences the picture of the world that he or she perceives.

The difference between the second and third approaches is as follows: The second approach states that we do not affect the world and that the picture of the world changes in our eyes because we change. The third approach, however, states that we do affect the world, that our perception of the world is a combination of the individual's qualities and those of the world. Today there are even some who claim that there are infinite possibilities, and the observer "chooses" which of them to perceive according to his or her attributes.

This last approach is rather close to the Kabbalistic approach. The fundamental difference between them is in the definition of "the existence of the world." Stating that the world has endless possible forms relies on the assumption that if I operate in a certain way the world will "react."

The Kabbalistic approach states that the world is totally abstract; it assumes no form whatsoever. There is nothing outside us but a never-changing, abstract Light. Even when we change with respect to the Light and perceive some of It, no change is induced in the Light itself. All that we perceive is our measure of internal congruence with the Light, nothing more.

From all we have said thus far we can see that our real life is very different from the way we perceive it. The picture of reality for each us depends entirely on our inner attributes. This picture is built of projections of our own attributes over the abstract Light.

Actually, the fact that our lives are an offshoot of what goes on within us bears profound implications: All the processes that we experience, even including life and death, are direct results of our vessels' perceptions. Moreover, it is in our hands to change them. Changing our vessels will allow us to switch from world to world and from reality to reality. We can then reach the highest levels of existence, where we are totally incorporated into the abstract Light.

## EXPERIENCING *EIN SOF*

The only difference between the vessels that perceive the corporeal reality and those that perceive the spiritual reality is in the intention. The corporeal vessels are egoistic and the spiritual vessels are altruistic. Intention is related to one's attitude towards the use one makes of one's desires.

The only state that really exists is the state of *Ein Sof* (Infinity). In that state, the Light is present within the *Kli*. However, that state is concealed, and the concealment prevents us from experiencing the state of *Ein Sof*. The altruistic intention gradually removes this concealment and exposes the Light that permanently fills the *Kli*.

If we keep this depiction in mind, we will remember that we never reveal any Lights outside the vessels. When Kabbalists say that Lights enter or exit the vessels, they wish to emphasize how one draws nearer to the attainment of the constant state. In Kabbalistic terms, *Ein Sof* is a state of "complete rest," meaning it is unchanging. Our work is to gradually prepare our tools of perception to perceive that state. Thus, the only change is in our abilities to perceive.

When Light "clothes" a person and one feels how it gradually enters, the constant state becomes gradually clearer as one awakens to feeling it. The Light never actually enters and never actually exits. It only becomes clearer and more evident, meaning more revealed and less concealed.

As Light becomes more evident in the *Kli*, it shows us that we are actually in the world *Ein Sof*, in the constant state, and that we must discover that this is our only state of existence. Thus, the Abstract Form doesn't exist at all. The Light that creates the *Kli* filled it immediately. There is no lapse between the making of the *Kli* and its filling. When Kabbalists say that Light emits from the Creator, they mean that there is already a *Kli* that is filled with It.

We must not forget that, unlike our time-related language, there is no time in spirituality. This is why we say that a *Kli* was first made and then filled. But in spirituality, these phases are simultaneous; the beginning and the end are at the same point.

Hence, the Abstract Form is really nonexistent, since the Form, or Light, is already clothed in its vessel. Our imagination can separate the Light from the *Kli*. We can assume that the Light within the *Kli* probably exists outside the *Kli* as well, although we have no perception of what is outside the *Kli*.

Let us try to demonstrate this concept: Assume there is a *Kli* in which I perceive the whole reality. Assume also that there is another *Kli* in which I perceive some of the reality, and one more *Kli* in which I cannot perceive anything. Correcting my vessels pertains to the expansion of my vessels from smaller to greater, and even greater. If I say that the Light fills my vessel, it does not mean that It did not fill it before, but that now I have discovered this reality in actual fact.

We can compare this process to an unconscious patient who is slowly regaining consciousness. His kin and friends surround him, waiting for him to wake up. As he slowly opens his eyes, he begins to recognize his whereabouts. From the patient's perspective, reality "came to him" and filled his vessel of sensation, because we measure everything from the perspective of the receiver.

The term, *Ein Sof*, does not pertain to anything outside the creatures. It pertains to the Thought of Creation. The final Form of the creatures is already present in the Thought of Creation. All creatures, none excluded, are already in that state with all their fillings. Our present state is therefore called "the imaginary state." We are that unconscious patient; we think that we exist in a certain way, and we are gradually awakening to see the actual reality. At the end of the process, every creature will be fully aware of its true state.

In his *Introduction to the Book of Zohar*, Baal HaSulam depicts three states that the souls experience in the process of their awakening to their true state. The first state is the beginning of Creation and contains everything that will later evolve. The second state is the birth of the souls. The third state is when souls obtain what was already present in the first state. In other words, the first state refers to the souls' potential existence; in the second, they are unconscious, and in the third they return to their original state.

We are accustomed to a modus operandi by which we first decide to do something, then execute our decision, and have the intended result at the end of the execution of our decision. However, the Creator is complete. Thus, for Him there is no difference between the decision and the execution. The concept of time does not apply to the Creator. This is why we say that in the Thought of Creation to do good to His creations, the beginning, the middle, and the end are integrated inseparably. It is only our perception that divides this Thought into three layers.

The concept of time applies to the creatures because we are uncorrected. Three states exist for us: (1) corruption, (2) preparation for correction and correction, (3) equivalence of Form, and filling. This sequence of actions creates our sense of time.

As *Reshimot* surface in us, they make us want and think various things. When the *Reshimo* changes, so does my thought. The difference between my thought a minute ago and my thought in the present creates the sensation that time is passing. When our thoughts and desires change slowly, we feel that time is "crawling." Conversely, when new thoughts and new desires pop up very quickly in our minds, we feel that time is "flying."

Upon acquiring the first spiritual degree, we feel that we are in a spiritual process, meaning a spiritual time. In that state, we no longer sense corporeal time and completely identify with the spiritual process, where time is measured by the changes and actions pertaining to our contact with the Creator.

The frequency of the to-and-fro "signals" from us (now Kabbalists) to Him creates the sensation of time. It is no longer a question of the number of years we spend in our physical bodies. When all the *Reshimot* have surfaced, are corrected, and are filled with all the Lights, alternating between states ceases. Because there are no more deficiencies to fill and we are in a state of wholeness, the sensations of time, space, and motion cease, as well.

## TO BUILD A HOUSE

Understanding the making of Creation can be simplified by an example: A person who wishes to build a house will first picture its final form. After that, one must carefully plan the work stages and then execute them.

This is not the case with the Creator. The minute the Creator thought about creating creatures, it was done, and they appeared in their corrected form. Thus, from the Creator's perspective, we are in our corrected form. It makes no difference that we discover our true state gradually.

Hence, when we want to receive strength, we turn to the state of *Ein Sof*, which we call "Creator." To receive strength and discernments, we turn to the corrected reality in which we already exist, and to which we must aspire. *Ein Sof* is the Thought, and the world *Atzilut* is the detailed blueprint—these are the two phases preceding the execution of the Thought. It is similar to the way one thinks about constructing a house and even puts one's thoughts in writing without having the materials.

Below the world *Atzilut* is the *Parsa*, the separation between the *Atzilut* and the world below it. The creatures begin from the *Parsa* downward.. Yet, the Creator does not have to wait for the creatures' actions. For Him, the Thought and the Blueprint are the whole reality. Below the *Parsa* exist the worlds *Beria*, *Yetzira*, *Assiya*, and below them is This World (Figure 14).

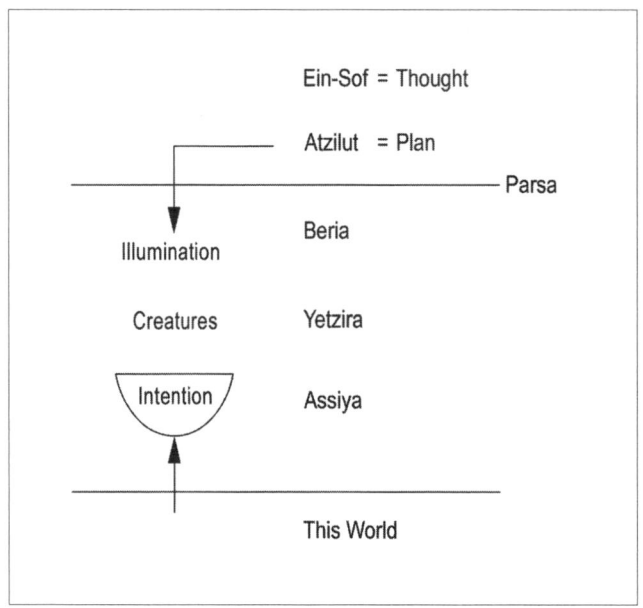

**Figure 14**

Light comes from the world *Atzilut* downward according to one's desire to "build the house." This desire, which one raises towards the Upper Light, is one's intention to please the Creator and resemble Him. In other words, it is the intention to obtain similarity with the Creator.

The process of bestowal upon the Creator consists of a beginning and an end. Not only do the beginning and the end pre-exist, but each of the intermediary stages exists as well. One knows the stages that one must go through in advance because, according to the blueprint, the pre-definition of each state stems from the *Kli* having to undergo a gradual correction.

There are diverse desires in the *Kli*, all of which are interconnected. They can be compared to organs in a single body, where each is required to build the intention to bestow. Correcting one desire influences all the others, which must unfold in their proper place in the correction order. There is nothing in one's life that is not predetermined by the structure of the will to receive, as the path of correction is predefined and divided into preordained orders.

We are always in the ultimate state, even now. As *Reshimot* surface and put us in varying states, all we do is realize each one. We cannot choose the states we will experience, but we *can* be assisted by the environment to realize the stages more effectively. Thus we will progress from one state to the next.

Moreover, even the way in which we realize the states we are placed in is predetermined. Nothing is new from the Creator's perspective; it is only hidden from us so we may independently choose to spiritually evolve. Later, when it no longer affects our efforts, we will discover that our successes and failures in achieving these states were also predetermined. When this occurs, we will be absolutely integrated in the Creator's perfect guidance.

If we were to correct beyond our interest in the results we feel in our vessels, we would no longer be influenced by what happens in the beginning, middle or end. Like the Creator, beginning, middle, and end would equalize in us and become one stage. This is why those who correct themselves transcend time and the effect of temporary stages. The correction we must undergo essentially consists of detaching from self-interest.

We can define a creature as "something" that feels itself detached from the Creator, and is ostensibly in its own right. From the point of view of the creature, the house isn't finished yet. The creature feels that it can contribute something to the building of it.

When the creature begins to want to discover the blueprint in order to complete the building of the house, the creature is considered to have brought itself back to *Ein Sof*. Its efforts to seek counsel and strength to understand the Creator's design and realize it bring the creature to ever-deepening familiarity with the plan, and to subsequent inclusion in the completed house.

Yet, this process unfolds precisely when the creature is seemingly adding every nut, bolt, board, and brick to the building. This addition constitutes one's *desire* to be incorporated in the house, not the actual construction of it. The raw materials, the metal, the wood, and the bricks are all desires. One need only want to place each desire in its proper place, according to the Creator's Plan. By building the house made of desires, one acquires the Creator's Thought. This is the creature's reward.

The Thought of Creation can only be reached from within this world. While being in this world, a Kabbalist gradually studies the actions of the Creator directly from Him and begins to want to do the same. Kabbalists called this process "from your actions we know you." The outcome of this process is the attainment of the Creator's Mind, His Thought.

The Thought of the Creator precedes the making of the creature. Hence, upon obtaining it, one not only brings oneself back to one's birthplace, but one rises even higher, transcending the level "creature" and reaching the actual level of the Creator.

At such a point we can say that they are of one mind, in adhesion, or equivalence of Form.

To be exact, the blueprint appears at the very first contact with spirituality. This is because each spiritual degree is a complete structure of ten *Sefirot*. The substance of the building, its structure, even its builder, all become known with the appearance of the very first picture.

After admission to the spiritual world, one becomes better and better acquainted with its structure because spirituality is built solely with one's consent to every step in the process. The consent pertains to one's intention to bestow, the altruistic intention. One's independence and free choice, one's "place of work," are in agreement with the altruistic intention. This is the addition that the Creator never added, nor can He add this.

The world *Ein Sof* is the house that the Creator so lovingly gives to the creature, but one must return the same love for Him, and by so doing seemingly build the same house for the Creator. Thus the creature returns the actions of the Creator, equalizes with Him, and hence elevates to the Thought of Creation.

## THE WORLDS ARE WITHIN

The Upper Worlds and their degrees exist only with respect to us, not in and of themselves. The worlds exist in potential, waiting for us to correct and discover their spiritual shape. In that state, we will immediately be presented with all the degrees between us and *Ein Sof*, beginning with the next adjacent degree.

A charge in a magnetic field "senses" the field's influence on it, and hence "knows" that the field exists. Had the charge not been inside the field, it would not have "felt" the effect of the magnetic field; in fact, it would not even know that the field exists.

Similarly, when leaving Earth's atmosphere, we discover that outer space is dark. It may sound strange, considering that sun-rays spread out across space, but if there is nothing that stands in the rays' way and "captures" them, we cannot detect the existence of the light.

Another good example of this principle can be observed when we watch sunlight come in through an open window into a room with some dust in the air. We can only detect the rays by their reflection off the dust in the air. In other words, if the crea-ture does not feel a certain thing, it cannot say that it exists on the outside. In such a state, we say that all that exists is the Thought of Creation to do good to that which has been created.

The creature, which is at *Ein Sof*, discovers the *Ein Sof* accord-ing to its relative correction or corruption. The degree of intensity in which it feels the Light in each of the spiritual levels, from *Ein Sof* to the creature, depends only on the individual creature. For this reason, we say that all the worlds are within each creature, and only after we perceive certain parts of the Thought of Cre-ation do we become aware of the existence of this Thought. We cannot talk about the Creator, attainment, or fulfillment when it is not from within the attaining individual, meaning if there is no *Kli*, there is no Light. In other words, without a creature, there is no Creator.

## ACCELERATING THE DEVELOPMENT

The Light of *Ein Sof* fills the whole reality, the entire will to receive that It created. It operates within it to bring it to equalize its form with Itself. The pressure of the Light on the will to receive is constant, unchanging in quantity or quality. In consequence, perpetual changes unfold in the will to receive, which we call "general providence," "from Above," meaning from the Creator to the creature. Because this attitude is permanent and unchang-ing, it is called "the *Ein Sof*, which is in complete rest."

The term, *Ein Sof,* emphasizes that the Creator is unchanging and that His purpose is also unchanging—to bring the creature to *Gmar Tikkun* (the End of Correction). Progression toward *Gmar Tikkun* is carried out through the Light's pressure on the *Kli,* which will eventually bring the *Kli* to feel that it is in contradiction with the Light's state.

Because of the pressure this creates, Kabbalists relate to this path as "the path of pain." While treading this path, everything happens in its due time, the constant pressure of the Light on the *Kli* inducing the making of diverse forms in the *Kli* until they are exhausted and the *Kli* reaches its *Gmar Tikkun.*

At the end of the natural evolution of the will to receive in humans, after many life cycles, one begins to feel that there is something higher, a Giver. At that phase, one begins to accumulate insights that do not belong to the will to receive, but to the will to bestow that pervaded the will to receive at the shattering of the vessels.

In such a state, one is between two forces—the will to bestow and the will to receive. Such a state allows one to accelerate one's development and progress faster than the natural pressure of the Light on the *Kli* would allow.

However, accelerating evolution toward the attribute of bestowal cannot be done from within one's ego. The only way to acquire the attribute of bestowal is to receive it from the Creator. The work of the individual is to find a way by which to receive the Form of bestowal "from Above," without having to fully experience the evils in the *Kli,* experiences that would force the creature to flee from reception to bestowal by pain and torment.

Choosing this path is called "evolution from below upward." In it, we walk *toward* the pressing Light and systematically bring upon ourselves all of the states, one by one. By taking this path, we want to progress toward the Creator, toward acquiring the Form of bestowal, and in so doing skip over the other states.

The great benefit of this alternative path, called "the path of Light," is that one experiences the same states, each and every desire, and its oppositeness from the Creator, but not because of the pressure from behind, but because of the craving for the Light. This path allows one to experience the necessary discernments quickly and in a more controlled manner. The path of Light is similar to discovering that we are ill, and taking the proper medicine *before* the illness actually breaks out. Thus, our own yearning can spare us great pain and troubles.

If we are drawn to the Light of our own accord; i.e., to the Forms of bestowal above the will to receive, we will skip terrible afflictions. This is why the wisdom of Kabbalah was given to humankind. Without it, humanity would progress naturally, step by step, each phase lasting until its negativity became fully exposed, and we would be forced into the next state. Teaching the wisdom of Kabbalah and how to use it to draw the Light will help us evolve in a very different way, pleasantly and quickly.

## BUILDING THE CREATOR WITHIN

As we have explained before, all the changes unfold within us, although they seem to be happening outside of us. We should understand that without experiencing that the changes are occurring outside us, we would not be able to make contact with the Creator or even think that the Creator exists and has any bearing on us. It is precisely this illusion that enables us to perceive the Light as something that exists outside of us.

When we relate what happens in us to the existence of an exterior Creator, we can build an attitude toward it and come to understand who the Creator is and how He wants to give to us. Had we not ascribed our inner experiences to the Creator, we would have been unable to perceive anything of Him. Moreover, we would have been unable to build the *intention* to bestow upon the Creator.

As we evolve, we gradually build a truer image of the Creator. At the end of the building process we reach the Simple Light, the Giver, the Ultimate Good, Who is in a state of eternal and unchanging love.

The illusionary sensation that there is a connection between the Creator and the creature changes according to the changes in the creature. This enables one to picture the Creator according to one's own attributes. In fact, in so doing one builds the Creator within; there is no other way to sense the Creator.

Projecting one's attributes upon the abstract Light illuminates the level above one's present level, which is the level that one pictures as the Creator. Thus, we refer the degree slightly higher than ours, which we will attain next, as the Creator. Once we have equalized with the attribute of bestowal on that degree, we "take" the place of the Creator. Now that person is in the place where the Creator was before (in our eyes).

Thus, as we evolve, we always picture the next degree through our corrupted attributes. We build the image of the Creator, which we aspire to become, in relation to our own attributes. This is the only way to perceive any Form of the Creator, the only way we can approach the abstract Light.

This imaginary sensation helps us build the present degree as well as the next degree. It facilitates our understanding of where to turn when we want to muster strength. Although it unfolds within, the image of the Creator that we build demonstrates the gap between our present state and the next state. Thus, we realize the difference between ourselves and the Creator. This is the only way to learn what is Above because the Creator has no Form that we can otherwise perceive. Hence, we build the Creator within us.

## PICTURING REALITY

We might compare a human being to a closed box with sensors: eyes, ears, nose, mouth, and hands, representing the five senses: sight, sound, smell, taste, and touch.

As we have previously said, the fundamental principle in perceiving reality is that of "equivalence of Form," which means equilibrium of pressures. The senses function as sensors, each with a different reaction to the pressure, depending on the make up of the sensor. The sight sensor evokes a reaction of light, darkness, and colors; the sound sensor evokes sounds; the smell sensor evokes scents; the taste, flavors; and the touch, sensations such as hard, soft, warm, and cold.

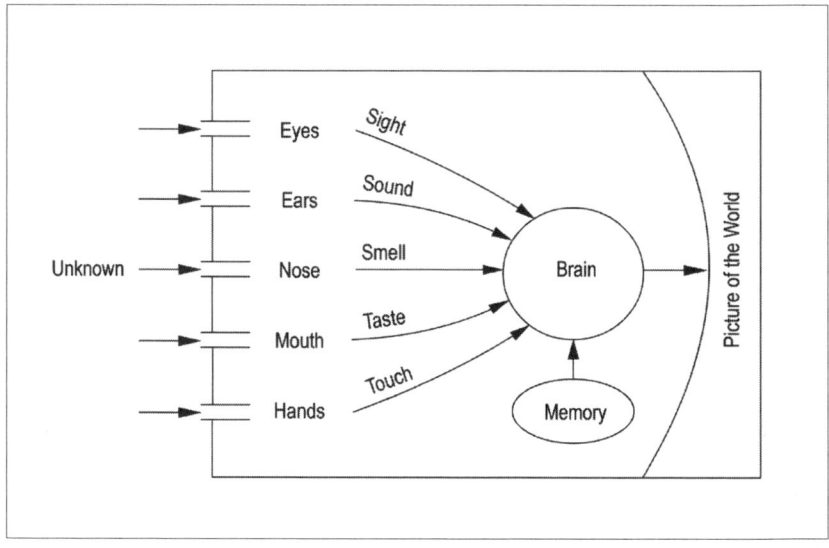

**Figure 15**

The reaction of the senses is transferred to the brain's control center, where the information is compared with the data that already exists in the memory, the reservoir of prior impressions. In this manner, we process what our senses gather, determine the most advantageous reaction, and study where we are and how best to function in our environment. When the process is completed, the information is "projected" unto a "screen" within the brain, portraying what is ostensibly in front of us (Figure 15).

In this process, the surrounding unknown becomes "known," and a picture of the external reality is created. However, the picture is not one of external reality, but merely an internal picture, a result of the structure of human senses and preexisting data. If we had different senses, we would produce an entirely different picture. Quite possibly, if we perceived through different senses, what appears as light would appear as dark, or even as something so fundamentally different that we cannot imagine how it would appear to us.

Science has known these facts for some time now. Today, we can replace senses using manmade means such as electronic devices. Although science has yet to fully master these techniques, in time it will be able to expand the reach of our senses, create new organs, and even produce a complete new body. Nevertheless, even with a new body, the pictures will remain within. Science has long since proven that the sensations of being in certain places and situations can be evoked through electric stimuli to the brain in conjunction with data stored in the memory.

All of the above teaches us that everything we feel comes from within, irrespective of our surrounding reality. We cannot even be certain that there *is* an outside reality. Because the picture of the "outside" world lies within us, Kabbalists refer to the world we see as "the imaginary world."

Everything is made of a desire to enjoy. In humans, this general desire to perpetually enjoy evokes desires to take pleasure in particular things, which change at any given moment. Combined with the information stored in the memory, this desire operates our senses toward what is momentarily desired. The evolution of the desire for pleasure throughout the generations eventually leads to a desire for something unknown called "the point in the heart." Today, this desire is awakening in many of us.

The problem with this desire is that there is no corresponding data that relates to it in our memory. Even the senses cannot locate a source of satisfaction for this new craving. When that desire arises in us, we stand helpless because there is nothing in the world around us that can satisfy it. But when this desire arises, it makes our lives prior to its appearance seem repellent.

The point in the heart is the beginning of an entirely new sensory system, completely detached from the present, natural system. When this new system is fully developed, it will be called "a soul." The soul will contain a new brain, a new memory, and a new "screen." Using it, one sees a whole new world-picture, that of the spiritual world. Thus, there are two separate sensory systems that operate similarly: the natural, corporeal system, and the spiritual system.

In the natural system, the world-picture appears at the moment of birth. We needn't do anything to create it, which is a substantial difference from the spiritual system. We experience many things through life, experiences that enrich and develop our memory, enhance our ability to process greater and greater subtleties, and make numerous interconnections and connotations. As a result, the picture created in our mind grows more and more lucid. This is the difference between the infant's perception of the world and the mature perception.

For the point in the heart to evolve into a system of spiritual perception, one must acquire a great desire for it. Since the spiritual world is hidden, the only way to intensify the desire for it is through the right environment. When one wants to progress spiritually, one is led to an appropriate environment, according to the measure of the will to receive. This is a natural process that happens as a result of the law of equivalence of Form, by which one is situated in the spiritual system according to one's desire to partake of it.

This environment comprises three elements: a Kabbalist guide, Kabbalistic texts, and a society of people with a similar desire. From this point on, one's evolution depends on one's desire to utilize this environment correctly, i.e. to enhance the desire for spirituality. When, and only when, the desire for spirituality grows to the required intensity to create another sensory system, the picture of the spiritual world will be created in that person.

This is the only purpose for which Kabbalistic texts were written. By correctly studying these texts, the construction of the soul is facilitated. Baal HaSulam (Kabbalist Rabbi Yehuda Ashlag) describes this in the following manner:

*Therefore we must ask, why then, did the Kabbalists obligate each person to study the wisdom of Kabbalah? Indeed there is a great thing in it, worthy of being publicized: There is a wonderful, invaluable remedy to those who engage in the wisdom of Kabbalah. Although they do not understand what they are learning, through the yearning and the great desire to understand what they are learning, they awaken upon themselves the Lights that surround their souls.*

*...when one engages in this wisdom, mentioning the names of the Lights and the vessels related to one's soul, they immediately shine upon us to a certain measure. However, they shine for him without clothing the interior of his soul for lack of the able vessels to receive them. Despite that, the illumination one receives time after time during the engagement draws upon one grace from above, imparting one with abundance of sanctity and purity, which bring one much closer to reaching perfection.*

~Baal HaSulam
*Introduction to the Study of Ten Sefirot, item 155*

Once the first picture of the new reality appears, the remainder of the evolution unfolds in a process the Kabbalists call "one's soul teaches one." The picture of the corporeal world becomes clearer as one matures and accumulates impressions. Here, too, one accumulates sensations and impressions of the spiritual world that enrich the new memory and analytic abilities of the new mind. Consequently, the world-picture created within the new sensory system becomes increasingly clearer.

The death of the biological body means that the natural system has ceased to function. The senses no longer transfer information to the brain, and the brain stops projecting the picture of the corporeal world on the "screen" within it. Since neither desires nor fulfillments in the point in the heart—from which the spiritual system evolved—belong to this world, this point continues to exist after the departure of the body.

If one has come to perceive one's existence in the spiritual system and has come to identify oneself with it before the demise of one's body, that person will continue to sense his or her spiritual existence past the death of the body. This is the meaning of existence in the soul.

\* \* \*

According to Kabbalists Baal HaSulam and the Holy Ari, to name just two, all that exists outside of us is the Light that fills the entire reality, and which is in complete rest. Although we are within that Light, we feel as if we exist inside a body situated within a surrounding universe.

Yet, as previously stated, impressions fill us through the five senses. Thus, if all that exists around us is the unchanging Light, what is it that makes us perceive constant changes?

To answer that question, we must return to the *Reshimot* (reminiscences). As we have said earlier, within the will to receive there is a chain of *Reshimot*, a chain that continuously evokes new *Reshimot*. The internal world-picture we experience is actually a manifestation of the difference, the contradiction between the presently active *Reshimo* (singular for *Reshimot*) and the Light.

The Light outside us does not change; only the *Reshimot* within us change. Our perception of ourselves and the world around us results from projecting the internally unfolding changes in our desire upon the constant, resting Light. The renewal of the *Reshimot* and the way one realizes them create our changing pictures of the world.

# Realizing
# the
# Spiritual Gene

# THE *RESHIMO*

Our perception of ourselves and reality determines how we sense ourselves and reality. This is the basis for all our research. We need to understand what a human being is, and if we have any existence in and of ourselves. Quantum physicists may be right when they argue that man, like all of matter, is merely a "bundle of waves." Perhaps the actual reality is very different from that which we presently see. However, if we can establish a fundamental, objective principle that will not depend upon our subjective sensation, a principle that defines "us" and defines "reality," we will have a standard by which to assess our present perception.

Many researchers believe that the more we progress in our research, the dimmer and vaguer we find things to be. They feel that we are groping in the dark. Our misunderstanding of ourselves and the world is at the core of the present global crisis we are facing. Without doubt, the scientific approach of researching the depths of reality is a good one, but we find there is a boundary, an impasse that we cannot penetrate.

Human nature, human perception, and everything science has discovered will not facilitate a forward movement. We will feel that from a certain point on, everything becomes "intangible" and "evaporates." This is what quantum physics is already beginning to discover--that matter is suddenly "lost," leaving researchers in a kind of vacuum.

A sensation of that sort stems from having lost the sense of the present reality, before having perceived the "approaching" Upper reality. This happens when one does not possess the tools to perceive that "other" reality. Baal HaSulam states (in his article, *The Essence of the Wisdom of Kabbalah*) that the only way to obtain that method is to learn from a Kabbalist who has already mastered it.

## A BLACKOUT

Our state in this world is far from our real state, from the standard we have mentioned above, called *Ein Sof*, where we are all connected as one desire filled with the Upper Light. The separation, or "exclusion," occurred to allow us to rise from the degree of desire to a higher degree than that of the desire itself, meaning the degree of intention. This enabled us to make free choices and acquire discernments and revelations with which we could transcend the creature-receiving degree and reach the Creator-giving degree.

Descending from the state of *Ein Sof* to the state of this world unfolds by dividing the single *Kli* into many particles. In spirituality, "exclusion" means "difference in qualities." By independently nearing the true state, we begin to understand the Thought of Creation, above the state of *Ein Sof*. Thus we are taught how to return to the state of *Ein Sof* by ourselves.

But for us to return to *Ein Sof*, we must first know the essence of that state. We are all in the state of *Ein Sof*, a state of love and mutual guarantee, forming a *Kli* to the Upper Light. To return from this world to *Ein Sof*, we must try to build a similar state in our interrelations. The *Ein Sof* is the truly existing state, though for the time being we are in an imaginary state with respect to our blurred senses. In other words, we are in the state of *Ein Sof* even now, but our senses are "veiled" with dust, which blurs our perception. We need to "clean up" our senses. Thus, the state of *Ein Sof* is the standard we are working to attain.

\* \* \*

We can never clearly understand a state while still in it. The present state becomes clearer only as we ascend to a higher state. The method of Kabbalah provides a new picture and outlook that enable us to understand our prior reality. Interestingly enough, we do not encounter many obstacles when dealing with the still, vegetative, and animate. Yet, when attending to matter at our own degree—the speaking—we invariably fail. Our helplessness in resolving the social and familial problems of our time is only one of many testimonials to that state.

The method of Kabbalah elevates us to a higher state than our present state. From this new perspective, we can see our former state and analyze it. This is the fundamental difference between the Kabbalistic mode of research and the ordinary scientific method. In scientific research, the researcher attempts to penetrate the same reality he or she is in, like a child trying to study what it means to be a child. In Kabbalah, however, the Kabbalistic researcher rises above the present level and studies the former, lower level.

Kabbalists do not engage in studying reality in the ordinary scientific manner. They do not try to broaden their narrow perception into a wider perspective because they do not think it is possible. Only correctly researching reality can facilitate our progress toward achieving the next steps. Without proper research, we will simply remain at the level of studying matter.

Proper research elevates the researcher to the level of the Forces that operate behind matter. When we perceive these Forces, we perceive what happens in matter as well, since these Forces become our own. The researcher senses these Forces as conducting his or her own life, at his or her disposal, perceived tangibly, through the senses, rather than intellectually.

One cannot research reality at a higher degree than nature scientists perceive using only rational and sensual perception. To move to a higher reality, one must change one's senses. Sophisticated research tools will not help here.

By studying nature, we can imagine a higher reality opposite to ours, where everything is aimed at giving instead of receiving. We can also assume that above our egoistic nature, everything operates with love and interconnectedness, that everything is actually a single Thought.

Scientists have found that all parts of reality are harmoniously connected, that each part helps the others and is vital in the collective system. The parts of reality are "considerate" with one another, as if cells of a single body. This finding brought researchers to hypothesize that the general law for every part of reality is the law of love. The only problem is that the researchers cannot raise themselves to that level and *be* that nature.

If scientists could change their nature in accordance with what they believe is present beyond the physical level, they would find that beyond the "hidden material" lies a very real, rock-solid reality, as real as the one they know now. They could perceive the Forces, their interconnections, and their systems. But for a researcher to discover all that, there must be congruence of form between the researcher and the level of these Forces.

We can compare this to walking into a completely dark room. First, we do not see the objects in the room, but if we switch on the light, we will be able to see them. Of course the objects were there to begin with, but our ability to perceive them was inadequate to the task. Thus, what we must do is match ourselves with the Forces that already exist in reality; and the way to match them is the method of Kabbalah.

## VIRTUAL REALITY

Numerous theories claim that there are endless realities existing simultaneously. Kabbalah states that there is only one. This reality is called *Malchut de Ein Sof*, meaning *Malchut* of the world *Ein Sof*. Nothing else exists. The term, *Malchut de Ein Sof*, designates the creature in its perfect and eternal state. Anything besides *Malchut de Ein Sof* is called "virtual reality."

The virtual reality consists of various images that appear before *Malchut de Ein Sof* as it declines into various degrees of "consciousness." In consequence, *Malchut de Ein Sof* feels less and less of itself and its filling.

The process of losing consciousness intensifies until *Malchut de Ein Sof* reaches its lowest, most turbid and detached state, called "this world." In that state, *Malchut de Ein Sof* takes the form of human souls that feel disconnected from one another. It is from this picture of reality that we must crave to return to the state of *Malchut de Ein Sof.*

By saying that our reality is virtual, we refer to the discernment that we make when discovering that this is how things stand. Perceiving such reality as virtual does not prevent us from working with it; we need only understand that this is one of the phases we must experience.

This can be compared to a child with lots of fantasies. The fantasies do not annul the child's world, and we know that these fantasies are appropriate for the child's stage of growth. Similarly, when entering a higher reality, we relate to the previous reality as though it were fictitious, though it is very real to those still at that level.

There is a kind of barrier between the spiritual reality and the corporeal reality. We cannot see the Forces behind this world until we cross the barrier, but these Forces depict the picture of the world within us in much the same way electric vectors create images on the TV or computer screen. When we look at the screen, we see a colorful, three-dimensional picture, but it is really nothing but a combination of electrical forces that can be processed, transferred, and stored. The truth is that we, too, exist in a similar picture, except that the screen is within us.

Those who rise to the level of these Forces see how real they are, while the picture they create is imaginary. These Forces constantly create different pictures, although the Forces themselves remain the same.

All in all, there are 125 degrees of attainment. The higher we rise in them, the truer and more correctly will we perceive how these forces connect. At the end of the ladder, one perceives the total merging of these Forces, called *Ein Sof*.

The principle that arises from this is that it is only when we attain and perceive something that we can define it. For this reason, all Kabbalists adhere to an unshakeable law stated by Baal HaSulam: "What we do not attain, we do not define by name or word."

## MASS MEDITATION

Many people tend to believe that humanity can improve its situation when it wishes to do so. One such example is mass meditations, often practiced throughout the world in order to raise our quality of life. Undoubtedly, connecting people in a single thought influences reality. The power of thought is indeed tremendous. However, we must understand that simply thinking about it will not induce any beneficial influence upon reality, much as we may want it.

Since our nature is egoistic, our best thoughts will still be focused on receiving better results for ourselves. Our situation will begin to improve only once we realize that our fundamentally egoistic nature is bad. If we understand that only by acquiring a new, altruistic nature can we be happy, then we will flourish and thrive. Such recognition will force us to replace our nature.

Actions such as mass meditation do not promote humanity to the Creator, meaning to the altruistic nature. They are predicated on our being able to maximize the use of our egoistic forces; hence, no single plan of humanity will help to improve our world. These actions will eventually lead to quicker disclosure of the evil in our egoism. In fact, any bonding of many people to achieve a common goal, positive or negative, accelerates the disclosure of evil, but this is not a desirable way for progress.

The optimal evolution occurs only when one draws "Light from Above." The spiritual Force exposes the flaws as well as corrects them, but to do that, there must be a method of correction. In the absence of such a method, humanity will be compelled to evolve through torment and affliction. Finally, the accumulated suffering will bring humanity to realize that it cannot do anything alone.

Drawing Light from Above is a result of the effort to be similar to the state of *Ein Sof*—the only state that truly exists, in which we are all connected as one standing opposite the Creator. We need not fantasize anything in an effort to resemble the final state because we are already in it. All we need is to want to receive the correction Force from that state, and that Force will bring us to actually be in it.

Kabbalistic texts depict the corrected state. If we read these texts and want to be in the corrected state, we thus "pull" in the Light in much the same way an unconscious person receives an IV. The Light operates on the reader, awakens, and helps one begin to climb.

We therefore see that the meaning of such terms as "Light" and "Above" is this: "Light" is the Upper Force that corrects and fills the creature; "Above" means "from a more corrected state, meaning a state of greater bestowal upon the Creator.

## WHAT IS THE CREATOR?

The Creator is what one finds to be the Upper Degree. The Hebrew term, *Boreh* (Creator), indicates an invitation to "come and see" (*Bo* means "come," *Re'eh* means "see"). One who attains the highest degree is in a state of adhesion with the Creator. Before reaching this highest degree, a flaw will always appear in this adhesion, although this is not really a flaw, but a new, uncorrected desire that has surfaced in the person.

These desires appear so that we will correct them, and through correction enhance our adhesion with the Creator. For every new desire that surfaces, the Creator seems higher than before. As one discovers the oppositeness of the Upper Degree and its level of altruism, one must muster the strength to elevate to it.

Hence, prior to the state of *Ein Sof*, where all the ends come together, there is no absolute Creator. The only definition we can give to the term, "Creator," is (until we reach *Ein Sof*) "higher than I am." The Upper Degree builds, creates, begets, corrects, and fills the lower degree.

The Creator appears as a blend of higher qualities than those one presently possesses. The *Reshimot* that awaken cause one to picture a higher degree every time. Nevertheless, the depiction of the Creator is always the projection of one's present qualities on the Abstract Light. The Abstract Light's pressure is constant; the changes and movements are only within. Although only the *Reshimot* change within us, it seems to us as if it is the Creator Who is changing.

## REALIZING THE *RESHIMOT*

A person who is not a Kabbalist realizes the surfacing *Reshimot* involuntarily. Such a person reacts according to the conditions in which he or she was placed: education, environment, internal forces, health and so on. In this manner, one is "taken" through various emotions and impressions and finally arrives at the desire for spirituality.

While progressing "despite self," one accumulates impressions from life's joys and sorrows, collecting discernments and using them along the way. This is a preparatory phase whereby one accumulates numerous impressions regarding one's will to receive, and experiences the realization of the *Reshimot* within.

Although we are unaware of it, all of these impressions remain in the brain, and when a certain *Reshimo* surfaces, the *Reshimot* that are necessary to realize it also awaken. We cannot control this process; events we experienced many years ago suddenly resurface and we cannot understand why.

Moreover, because souls are interconnected in a single system, each "personal" impression of a person, or a group of persons, affects every other soul. Processes that unfold in a certain place on Earth affect all Earth's inhabitants, even if they are unaware of it. We are presently unable to understand how this information is transmitted, but it becomes crystal clear upon obtaining the state of *Ein Sof*. We accelerate the emergence of the *Reshimot* because we are parts of a single system.

We all exist as one creature with respect to the Upper Light; each of us is comprised of all the others. Each is like a single *Kli* that the Creator created as a hologram, and each person is comprised of the "self" and its incorporation, or existence, in all the other souls. The incorporation of a person into all other souls is bidirectional, meaning one is within the other souls, and the souls are within that person. This is why the will to receive contains so many discernments and changes.

There is always contact between the Upper Light and the individual, but one's connection to this contact varies. The Upper Light shines upon the desires within us, evoking a sensation that we call "the picture of my world," whether it is this world or the spiritual world. This sensation changes constantly under the influence of one's own *Reshimo*, as well one's integration in *Reshimot* of other souls. The sum of these changes creates one's dynamic picture of life.

## CHOOSING THE FUTURE

We believe that we have many possible futures to choose from. But choosing means seeing the future, so what is this choice based on? How does one know which future is best? If we could see the result of choosing one option and the result of choosing another option, we would know which was better. But in truth, there are no options to choose from whatsoever.

A certain *Reshimo* awakens within a certain will to receive, meaning within a certain person situated in a certain environment. Subsequently, that person realizes the *Reshimo*, accumulating further impressions from life's events.

If we realized that we are only marionettes, and that at the same time we *can* change our future, we would then be at a point of choice. In other words, we could then choose an environment that would influence us positively and assist in our spiritual development. Such an environment would help us realize that *Reshimo* in the same direction and the same preexisting ladder, but we would do it willingly, instead of under pressure.

In any given state, the *Reshimo* in the awakened will to receive, and the environment are all predetermined. Even if one had an urge to realize the *Reshimo*, this urge would stem from within; and even if one used the environment to accelerate the unfolding of the *Reshimo*, it would only shorten the predetermined unfolding period.

However, our efforts to be part of an environment that is interested in spiritual evolution, and to be prompted by it to evolve, offer us a new intellect—"the comprehensive intellect," which pertains to the Creator's intention with respect to the creatures. Acquiring that intellect means discovering that intention and the subsequent ascent to the Creator's degree. This is the great bonus.

We need to understand that, by ourselves, we can want any-thing except to advance in the right way to the right goal. A per-son alone is like a blind person—unable to see the path of correct progress. We cannot see the outlet from this world to the Upper World, from the will to receive to the will to bestow. We cannot even see that such a thing exists and that here lies our salvation.

It follows that the point of free choice is very, very subtle. We can choose an environment that will bring us to a state where the Upper Light changes our quality, and through the operation of that Light, we will be able to enter the spiritual realm. But alone, without a method or a social environment, we cannot make the breakthrough to spirituality.

* * *

Terms such as "parallel worlds" and "parallel universes" are becoming increasingly fashionable. Many find the possibility of choosing their future enchanting. There are meditations that of-fer abilities to choose first thing in the morning the events of the coming day. Psychologically speaking, in this manner one is "programming" oneself and predetermining a specific manner in which to accept the *Reshimot* that will surface that day. Yet the question remains whether or not we can actually create a different reality by doing this.

We cannot say that such a person is exceptional, as we all have our predispositions about life. We all have habits with which we start our day, whether they are physical exercise or a visit to a therapist.

Whether we plan our day consciously or unconsciously, the fact remains that our picture of reality is entirely determined by the *Reshimo* within us. This *Reshimo* situates us in this picture and creates all the decisions in it. Correspondingly, our conscious ef-forts to "choose" what will happen are a product of the unfolding *Reshimo*, and nothing more.

## THE MEMORY

All of the pictures that make up our lives are connected to one another. Thus, evoking a certain *Reshimo* often reminds us of past experiences. We do not manage our memories, nor can we draw anything from them or forget others. The *Reshimo* determines absolutely everything. We only move "atop" the experiences that awaken and work within us. If a realization of a *Reshimo* requires it, past memories will pop up on their own.

Everything we ever experienced remains within us; nothing ever disappears. A *Reshimo* that awakens in one's desire is then realized opposite the Light and produces a discernment of what is happening at that moment. Subsequently, another *Reshimo* awakens, and since the *Reshimot* are connected, the new *Reshimo* uses the old *Reshimo* according to its need.

When several other *Reshimot* have come and gone, the first *Reshimo* is lost from memory and the pictures it created dissolve from sensation. These sensations might later reawaken if they are needed for the realization of a new *Reshimo*. Thus we discern a chain of experiences in which the *Reshimot* become active and passive, and as these *Reshimot* are realized, they accumulate impressions within us.

This process unfolds "Above" us; hence we cannot approach our memory and draw specific pictures from it. For example, while walking on the street we might encounter a familiar scent that briefly reminds us of a childhood scene. As the scene appears, it disappears, and we cannot understand its purpose. However, nothing is accidental in the world; all the memories surface only according to their necessity for the realization of the present *Reshimo*.

All souls are connected within a single, comprehensive system. We can therefore say that memory, too, is common to all of them. This becomes increasingly clear as one becomes more connected to every other soul. The more we consciously work toward this system, more memories will surface in us, and along with them, collective abilities and attainments. If we rise to a degree of bonding with others and work with their vessels as though they were our own, we will certainly utilize everything within them.

## THE POWER OF THOUGHT

Thought is a very powerful force. In the docudrama, *What the Bleep Do We Know?*, Dr. John Hagelin told of an experiment in mass meditation carried out in Washington, D.C.. According to Hagelin, it turned out that mass meditation on reducing crime levels in Washington D.C. yielded impressive results and crime level dropped by twenty-five percent that summer.

Yet, in this act there is still no free choice, since it is the *Reshimo* that performs the whole process—the decision to carry out the mass meditation, as well as the subsequent decrease in crime level. Regardless, at present we wish to work with only the modus operandi of human desires, not the degree above it, which "manages" us.

Bringing a group of people together with a single goal creates a great power. This is so because everyone unconsciously uses the already existing system in which they are already connected. Even if people bond for the worst of goals, they will awaken tremendous powers.

Thoughts change reality because a thought is an expression of the desire. By wanting reality to be one way or another, we seemingly channel our future in the desirable direction.

If crime levels are due to rise and thousands of people bond in meditation to lower them, they will decrease because the participants in the experiment inserted their will into that *Reshimo*. The *Reshimo* is crude potential, and one's attitude toward the *Reshimo* can affect the form the *Reshimo* will take.

Bonding people in common thought creates congruence with the state of *Ein Sof,* where all the souls are already connected. We should state that such congruence exists even when the bonding is not carried out to approach the Creator, i.e. bestowal. In other words, congruence with the system works regardless of its connection to the Creator. Bonding draws power from Above, which changes the way the *Reshimo* seems to unfold. Yet, we must keep in mind that our attitudes towards the *Reshimo* are also predetermined within the *Reshimo.*

Let us use the mass meditation example to clarify the subtle issue of free choice. Two points need to be emphasized:

- After the awakening of a desire to use the collective power, one applies this power and reaches an impressive result.

- Activating the desire yields a substantial result because that person utilized the *Reshimo,* the system, and the Light.

Truthfully, there is not a single act in all of this that stems from the individual, since the *Reshimo* prodded that person into action. As with any other machine, the person performed an act and yielded a certain outcome. The only involvement of the individual in the process was the documenting of the causes and the consequences. In fact, because we acquire independent existence in spirituality, our knowledge is nothing more than recording causes and consequences.

## THE CHAIN OF *RESHIMOT*

Our perception of reality is our sensation of the Upper Light. The measures of sensing the Light are called "this world" or "the spiritual world." This world pertains to a sensation of the Upper Light via an egoistic intention, while sensing the world via an altruistic intention is called "the spiritual world." These depictions express two forms of relation toward the Upper Light.

Our attitude toward the Upper Light defines our state; it determines in which world and in what degree we are situated. This attitude is determined by the *Reshimot* that evolve from zero degree onward. These *Reshimot* evolve by a certain order, starting with the still, through the vegetative, animate, and up to the physical speaking, the human. The speaking degree continues to evolve through interior degrees of still, vegetative, animate, and (spiritual) speaking. The chain of *Reshimot* determines everything, and besides that nothing exists.

The *Reshimot* evoke increasingly stronger desires in us, starting with physical-existential desires (for sex, food, and family), through desires for wealth, honor, domination, and ending in a desire for knowledge.

Scientists work with the highest desires in the human species—desires (*Reshimot*) for knowledge and erudition. Once we exhaust all the *Reshimot* in the egoistic desire to receive, we are required to commence our correction in order to progress onward.

Kabbalah begins where our ability to research reality ends. This is so because the wisdom of Kabbalah enables one to change a *Reshimo* from egoistic to altruistic. Realizing a *Reshimo* altruistically allows the researcher to transcend the realization level of the *Reshimot* that awaken in the researcher, which brings us to the level of the Forces that coordinate the elicitation of the *Reshimot* into the spiritual world. In the spiritual world, the researcher explores the Forces that form the Roots of that person's virtual reality, the very Forces that scientists so desperately seek.

Scientists are at the highest evolutionary level of desires in this world. This is precisely their plight: they cannot find the root of everything or learn what happens beyond matter. They do succeed in assuming that there is a Thought past matter, and that this

Thought is probably one of love and giving. They will even come to state openly that there must be a different way to research reality; alas, they will not be able to find it. It is impossible to change the innate approach to the realization of the *Reshimot* without the wisdom of Kabbalah.

Humanity doubtless had to realize all the *Reshimot* up to its present state without being consulted in the matter. But today, humanity finds within itself a craving to know the reason for its desperate state; the outcry that surfaces from the heart of humanity invokes the disclosure of the wisdom of Kabbalah. Kabbalah will help humankind realize the spiritual *Reshimot* to which it is now shifting, the *Reshimot* that prompt the intensifying spiritual quest of so many people.

If humanity waits until its researchers reach the truth on their own, without the assistance of the wisdom of Kabbalah, it might find itself in an unprecedented avalanche of crises, failures, and disasters. This is why the wisdom of Kabbalah is surfacing now, to ease the transition. This is also what Kabbalists have been trying to explain to humanity before it falls into these predicaments.

# REVEALED AND CONCEALED

The difference between the revealed and the concealed in this world and the spiritual world is only with respect to us. Everything we still do not know—in this world, as well—is called "concealed." If what is unknown becomes known, it becomes revealed. Thus, at any given moment we are in both the revealed and the concealed. The difference between this world and the spiritual world is in the way we acquire forms and patterns of perceiving reality.

The spiritual world is a reality where the patterns to perceive it do not come naturally, from within us or from the environment. Because the spiritual reality abides by opposite laws than our natural laws, where we presently exist, the spiritual world requires that we invert our attitudes. But where can we find the "opposite" strength to build "opposite forms"? If we are naturally built to build egoistic forms, how will we be able to build within us any altruistic forms and perceive the altruistic reality?

Such an inversion requires a special process, called *Segula* (merit). *Segula* refers to an indirect process that traverses the Upper System, and then returns to the individual. Using Kabbalah studies, one draws nearer to the Upper, altruistic Thought. This Thought does not act upon the will to receive, or upon the ego, but rather on the altruistic point—the point in the heart.

The similarity of nature between the point in the heart and the Upper Thought creates a connection between them, and they possess the same nature. The Upper Thought acts upon the point and molds it into various patterns, which we perceive as seeming to exist outside of us, in the spiritual realm.

Actually, these Forms do not exist outside of us at all, but within us. As with the illusion that everything we see in this world is outside us, so is the case in the spiritual world. However, when we acquire more spiritual Forms, we come to understand and to know the Thought that develops and builds these Forms within us.

During the process of coming to know this Thought, we build internal Forms that become increasingly similar to the Upper Thought. In so doing, we equalize ourselves with this Thought until it becomes the "self" of that person, after which one rises to the level where this Thought originated.

## INVERTED WORLD

The Upper Force creates the entire picture of reality within us—our nature, character, health, wishes and thoughts, and even our friends, country, and the world we live in. All this is prepared by the Upper Force. Everything that happens within us and around us is intended to bring us to a single resolution: to bond with this force.

But if this is how things are, we should ask, "How could this so-called benevolent Upper Force create such a harsh and bitter reality as we see before us?" In that regard, Kabbalists said, "He who charges others, charges with his own fault." The world picture is completely personal and entirely affected by the level of correction of one's attributes.

In the article, Concealment and Disclosure of the Face, Baal HaSulam expounds on the meaning of changing one's perspective, changing one's tools of perception. In this article, Baal HaSulam argues that perceiving phenomena from the perspective of the correction is opposite to perceiving phenomena from the perspective of the corruption. Through egoistic vessels, it seems as though egoists succeed; through altruistic vessels, they seem to be suffering. But did these people actually change? Did they fall from riches to rags, from bliss to anguish? Moreover, can our correction change the state of those we observe?

One who senses the spiritual reality and observes the corporeal reality, perceives its events and incidents differently than one who does not sense spirituality. Such a person sees only how the egoistic actions performed in our world are untruthful, noxious, and create distance between their doers and the Upper Force.

The more enjoyable and fulfilling a phenomenon is thought to be (in egoistic vessels), the farther it is from the nature of the Upper Force in the eyes of one who feels the spiritual reality. In such a state, that person will perceive it as more afflictive since it distances that individual from the Upper Force and the quality of bestowal.

## CONTRADICTORY PHENOMENA

It seems hard to believe that researchers would agree to the statement that "we create the world-picture before our eyes." This is because that would mean that there is nothing more to research. and researchers are customarily regarded as people who aspire to change the world. But changing the world is impossible using the traditional methods of research. At this point, Kabbalah provides researchers with tools that will enable them to research themselves, and thus change the world.

In other words, Kabbalah will assist an honest researcher to achieve what he or she wanted from the beginning—to change the world. However, the change will be internal, not external. The wisdom of Kabbalah will enable science and human perception to evolve into the next phase, beyond time, space, and motion. In that state, all the phenomena that today appear contradictory to researchers will merge.

Now we can also understand how our desires gradually evolve. Having developed from desires to wealth to desires for honor and domination, and finally to the desire for knowledge, it is now time for the desire for spirituality, the desire that induces our exposure of the wisdom of Kabbalah.

A scientist who studies the wisdom of Kabbalah is acquainted with the foundation of Creation. Such a scientist will be surprised to discover how tightly matters are connected to the rules discovered in the material world. Subsequently, this congruence between spiritual laws and physical laws will help the researcher to resolve problems in every field of contemporary life.

In ecology, psychology, social or political science, in every field of science we are faced with the absence of the "right formulae." Things did not use to be so complex. In Newton's time, for example, discovering only a few formulae sufficed to explain everything. But today we have climbed to a new level of research in matter; at this level, we lack the formula that explains the general conduct of matters.

If science claims to engage in humans and the world they live in, Kabbalah states that in all our fields of research, we actually research ourselves, not the world around us. In physics, chemistry, physiology, ecology, or any other science, we research not the outside world, but our *inner* world, our inner vessels. Modern science is discovering that traditional research has exhausted itself. All that is needed now is to see that the entire world is actually within us.

## A NEW SCIENCE

The realities we cannot see today, illiteracy of the affect of thoughts, inability to get along with society and with the environment, are all consequences of the erroneous premise that the world exists outside of us. This is why we are unable to formulate clear, sustainable rules that provide secure and safe sustenance. We must understand that we judge everything from within; if researchers agree to that, it will mark the beginning of the new science.

The new science will facilitate a clear understanding of the world we live in and make a proper connection to reality. To bring the method of correction to humanity, we must adopt the viewpoint that we exist within ourselves. Admittedly, changing attitudes towards the perception of reality is no small matter, especially with such fundamental change as the one we face today. In the past, when new methods came about they always required time to be accepted.

Hardest of all is the transition to the new perception, because according to the new perception, nothing exists but the perceiving individual. All former perceptions argued that there is something outside us with which we connect, whether in thought or in action. The argument that the human being is the Creator's sole creation, and that, besides the perceiving individual, there is only the Upper Light, is difficult to comprehend.

The understanding that all we feel are internal phenomena is not a psychological switch. Rather, it is a fundamental change that forces us to delve within. One cannot merely agree with the new perception, but must cultivate and improve one's inner qualities to finally equalize their form with the Upper Light on the outside. When one's qualities change and are no longer opposite from the Creator's qualities, one begins to discover the Creator. In that state, one becomes "transparent" with respect to the Upper Light, and the human matter—the will to receive—no longer acts as a partition before the Light.

* * *

Kabbalah explains that our tools of perception are comprised of five parts; three of these parts are called "internal vessels" and the other two are called "external vessels." With the internal vessels we feel ourselves, and with external vessels we feel our surrounding world. The external vessels create the sensation of an external reality because they are incomplete vessels, insufficiently developed.

When one corrects one's vessels (including the external vessels) in the fullest measure, the external world, too, will be felt as internal. Thus, the outside world will disappear and will become the simple Light that fills the whole reality. Since the correcting person has equalized with the Upper Light in every quality by annulling all the differences between them, that person is now in reciprocal perception with the Upper Light. This state is called *Dvekut* (adhesion), a state where one is totally integrated in the Upper Light.

\* \* \*

The difference discovered by quantum physics between the behavior of matter as a particle and its behavior as a wave is tantamount to the gap between matter—the will to receive—and the Light. Through Kabbalah, humanity will come to know the purpose for which matter is required to arrive, namely equivalence of Form between matter and Light.

At that time, there will be no difference, from our perspective, between a wave and a particle, or between Light and matter. We are presently incapable of comparing two contradictory things and situating them under the same roof. Only when one determines that reality is within and that there is nothing without, only if one lets go of the perception of "me" and "outside of me," will these opposites become as one.

# NATURE'S LAWS

We live in a world we know only partially. There are many rules in Nature, some of which we discover easily because they are evident from our own existence. The law of gravity, for instance, is evident because when we try to fly without the proper instruments we fall right back to Earth.

Some laws apply only to Earth and some also apply to space. Some of these rules are perceived through our senses and our bodies, but there are other laws, such as the laws of radiation, whose action we cannot feel. We can only see the phenomena they produce. We cannot perceive, hear, or see waves, but we do recognize their effects.

There are other rules whose effects we do not know. At times we feel certain phenomena, but we cannot clearly identify their origins. Either way, our experiences demonstrate that if we knew all the rules that affect the world, we might be happy and successful.

Some rules we learn from experience, some rules of behavior children pick up from their parents, their friends, the environment, and the general society. The rules we learn by education are not innately known to us. It is not clear that this is how they actually exist in the world, but our educators persuade us in various ways that it is so, and that this is a path worth treading. If children could see for themselves that something was wrong, they would not do it.

If one does not understand personally that it is bad to be cruel and evil to others, if one fails to see that theft is a negative phenomenon, society demonstrates this by penalties it attaches to such actions.

If we were aware that there was a law of reality that determined that if we stole, nature would respond with a negative reaction, we would not do it to begin with. If we knew that the penalty for stealing was illness or that something terrible would happen to us or to our loved ones, we would avoid stealing. Thus, where one does not see the law and the consequences of one's actions, society helps determine the rules one must follow, along with the system of reward and punishment.

Clearly, we would like to know how the natural rules operate and then behave accordingly, but the rules pertaining to our relationship with society and with the Upper Force seem to be hidden. Kabbalah states that these rules can be followed only once they are attained. When humankind reveals the whole system and understands the connection with the Upper Force, we will certainly be able to follow the general law of reality—the law of bestowal. But until then we cannot force anyone into such a state.

* * *

In Kabbalah, the numeric value of the words "God" and "Nature" is the same (86). Stating their equality emphasizes that all of nature around us, this world as well as the upper, spiritual worlds, are all God. The system of these forces is the manifestation of the Creator before us.

We know the rules at the physical level, and perhaps we will know additional laws in several hundred years, but this is not the source of our problem. As we evolve, we must come to know the spiritual laws, those that pertain to the human degree in us.

Presently, not only do we not know them, we are not even close to knowing them. Consequently, humanity falls deeper into predicaments generation-by-generation, and our situation is growing more desperate. None of the physical laws that we will discover in physics, chemistry, biology or any other field of science will be of help to us. Using scientific discoveries to benefit humankind will not make our lives any better, safer or more complete, since we are not keeping the spiritual rules.

What have we gained by learning how to grow more crops if human egoism prevents us from dispensing them to everyone's benefit? Human beings use every benefit from the rules they have discovered against themselves because they have not corrected themselves as humans. We suffer because we do not know how to conduct the speaking, human degree within us. All humanity's problems stem from the single fact that we do not conduct ourselves correctly.

People kill one another, they are frustrated, afraid, and desperate. All those phenomena are the maladies of the speaking degree within us, not those of the still, vegetative, or animate degrees in us. We do not feel bad about anything that pertains to the still, vegetative, and animate degrees in us.

We have food, water, and shelter. To past generations living conditions were much harsher, but people were happier. We are not happy, and it all stems from the imbalance between the speaking degree in us and nature's forces. This state will not change unless we change, study these forces, and equalize with them.

We are like a screw in a perpetually working engine. If we are not at exactly the right position, if we are not in sync with the machine, we are certain to feel discomfort. The fact that we are not rushing to correct our position with respect to these forces may ultimately turn against us. A thousand or two thousand years ago humanity was not so opposite to nature's machine. But today we are more evolved, more egoistic, crueler, and hence in greater contrast to nature's laws. Baal HaSulam says that this is the reason that our suffering intensifies with every generation.

...nature, like a competent judge, punishes us according to our development, for we can see that to the extent that mankind develops, so increase the pains and torments... And besides the blows we take today, we must also consider the drawn sword for the future, and the right con-

*clusion must be drawn, that nature will ultimately defeat us and we will all be compelled to join hands in following of the commandments with all the required measure.*

~Baal HaSulam

*The Peace*

The system of laws operates on us incessantly; it does not ask our opinion in the matter. If we know it, we will get along with it and have a blissful life. But if we do not study, we will feel greater discomfort the more we continue to evolve and fall behind in balancing ourselves with the system.

To discover the spiritual rules, we must begin to change ourselves and operate in accordance with these rules. This is why we have been given the wisdom of Kabbalah. Thus, the sciences we have known and developed thus far relate to the inanimate nature, to the vegetative and the animate levels, and the wisdom of Kabbalah is surfacing in relation to the speaking, human level.

# KABBALAH–THE MODERN SCIENCE

Unlike any other science, Kabbalah reveals to us the Upper World. This is why it is most often referred to as a "wisdom" instead of a "science." The empiric, scientific approach of the wisdom of Kabbalah is based on the same research principles that apply to other fields of research. Kabbalah, too, regards the observer as the researcher and studies reality as it is sensed by a human being, from a subjective perspective. The uniqueness of the wisdom of Kabbalah compared to any other fields of human study is that the subject of its research is the higher part of reality.

The wisdom of Kabbalah enables one to attain the roots of reality, not just another segment of the whole, but reality at its highest levels, before we ever reached it. Attaining the roots of reality grants researchers control over events before they clothe in our world, and the ability to interfere and change them, to lead and guide them using their unique approach.

If we determine our desire in such a way that the entire reality will appear to us in the direction of bestowal upon the Creator, if we want to live in a reality where the five senses are devoted to a single aim, to delight the Creator, then in that state we will determine our attitude to reality in the realm and at the level of the "sixth sense." This means holding an altruistic attitude to reality, which yields an entirely different characteristic to the reality perceived through the five senses. We will no longer attain a mere speck of reality, but its very root, ascending to the control room, the headquarters of reality.

In so doing we can rise above the creature level and reach the Creator's degree, the Source from which the Upper Forces comes and clothes the mundane matter. If we change our attitude to the forces while they are still at their root, we will feel their clothing in our world entirely differently. The empty sensation will yield before the sensation of the Upper Light.

Reality advances incessantly toward the revelation of the Creator to the creatures. It all depends on one's attitude to reality. If the creature progresses toward this goal willingly, through resembling oneself to the Creator, that person will experience the revelation of the Creator as an increasing flow of abundance. Conversely, if the revelation of the Creator unfolds unwillingly, meaning when the creature does not exert to resemble the Creator, the revelation will be perceived as threatening and evil, induced by the disparity of form between the egoistic individual and the upper bounty, whose nature is bestowal.

Disclosure of the Creator in a state of disparity of form brings darkness to one's life. This darkness is the "back side" of the Upper Light. The Upper Light already fills us, but we are presently unable to discover it, and the appearance of the darkness serves as a clarion that invites us to change our attitude to reality and discover the Upper Light.

The sixth sense is not added to the five senses; rather it stands above them, separately. Just as our will to receive perceives the corporeal reality with five modes of perception, which are our five senses, so our sixth sense comprises five modes of perception of the higher reality. With the help of the sixth sense, another reality is felt in the five senses, and this is the transition from darkness to light, from emptiness, fear, and torment, to abundance, security, tranquility, eternity, and perfection.

Acquiring the sixth sense expands our knowledge through positive impressions of abundance. When we acquire this sense, the Upper Light appears as profusion that fills the vessels, instead of as darkness. This new state will change the result of research in science. Physicists, chemists, and biologists will receive new results in their researches, as though finding the other side of the coin. Humankind will stop researching afflicted vessels devoid of Light, and instead will thrive and flourish toward the Creator's Light with a will that is truly free.

Such existence will be existence from the perspective of the Light, the perspective of a corrected *Kli*, since with the altruistic aim the *Kli* becomes Light and acquires the form and attributes of the Light. Humanity will develop sciences through utilizing the sixth sense—the altruistic intention. Drawing Light by equalizing with It will expose humankind to a different existence of Nature, existence in the positive, not the negative.

All levels of existence are contained within man; they rise and fall along with him. If a person becomes a "real" human, similar to the Creator, all of nature—inanimate, vegetative, and animate—receive a different nourishment and fulfillment. When humankind resembles the Creator, this world will be incorporated in the worlds *Beria*, *Yetzira*, and *Assiya*, and will rise along with them to *Ein Sof*. All of Nature will then rise and bond with the Creator.

In the egoistic and corrupted state, one does not see that the picture of reality is empty and lacks the presence of the Creator in it. The Creator appears as the provider of reality along with the acquisition of the sixth sense. He appears as the one who is inside reality's every detail, and in consequence, one's sensations in the five senses testify to that state, as though they are a gift from the Creator. In that state, the world appears as the measure of one's contact with the Creator, as the bonding measure between the individual and the Creator.

The more one senses the Creator as clothed in reality, the more one discovers that the Creator is within oneself and directs one's senses toward that sensation, and the more one loses oneself. All that remains is a tiny point where one stands as an observer, watching the revelation of the Creator from within and from without. This is why Kabbalists said that the Creator created the *Kli*, as well as filled it with the picture of the world.

It is precisely through the sensation of the "absence of self" that an opportunity opens before one to determine oneself. It is exactly at this point that one can determine one's independent attitude toward reality.

Through discerning that the *Kli* is not one's own, that its filling is not ascribed to oneself, one begins to discern one's ability to determine one's attitude to reality. At this point one begins to cultivate the sixth sense, above the five senses, the sense in which one establishes one's self. From the perspective of the *Kli*, a person decides how to feel the filling in the *Kli*, determining one's identity with respect to the filling. This is how a person grows in whom the erupting evolution is called "the wisdom of Kabbalah."

We therefore see that the science humanity is nurturing via the five senses is but a fraction of the comprehensive picture of reality. Many changes will unfold in science and its research boundaries will expand far beyond the present knowledge and discoveries. The fraction of reality that humanity has already discovered was discovered from within the empty vessels, not from the wealth that appears in corrected vessels. The scientists' recognition of the impasse they have reached is actually the acknowledgement of the empty vessels. Humanity has discovered all it could discover in these vessels, while the Light is still absent in the *Kli*.

Human science and all its branches are accumulation of knowledge from a position of absence of abundance. Science, like every other human engagement, demonstrates the negativity and the inability to evolve. Today, an absence of abundance in the vessels is leading to increasing despair. Human beings acknowledge that all the mundane pleasures—sex, food, family, wealth, honor, power and knowledge—offer no fulfillment and leave us empty. This emptiness is the driving force behind the desire to reveal the Upper Science—the wisdom of Kabbalah.

Many scientists and philosophers admit that they relate to the world as to a real threat. From their point of view, humanity has lost both control and the understanding of where it is headed. Only a few years are left for humanity to continue to evolve before it stands at the brink of a chasm that will eliminate every aspect of human life: ecology, society, economy and culture, research and education. These scientists already understand that without discovering the Thought, the Essence that generates matter, science will not be able to progress. They give humanity only a few years to evolve and say that humanity is presently facing an unprecedented crisis.

Humanity has known predicaments before, but they had always appeared in a single realm of human life: religion, culture, industry, or science. When one realm fell, another rose in its place; new ideologies replaced the old, and the world moved on to new eras. Today, however, all of humanity's engagements have reached total negation.

Humanity seems to be turning to religion, as it has done before science, industrialism and culture took its place. In truth, this time around it is a very different unfolding. The worldwide upsurge of religions and mystic teachings of all sorts is not due to their strong appeal to people, but for lack of choices.

Humanity is losing hope that science and technology will improve its state and sweeten its bitter life. The reason for the new attraction to religion is to test once more, learn once again, and for the last time, that no cure and relief for our present crisis will be found in them.

Religions design theories and philosophies that argue that science and religion can be combined and thus improve our lives. But this notion too will prove mistaken. The renewed interest in religion is also the last. It will lead to the recognition of religion's inability to provide a true answer to the empty vessels that will surface.

Thus, all the processes unfolding today summarize millennia of human evolution in egoistic vessels. From here on we must cultivate new vessels, altruistic ones. These vessels will display before us an entirely different reality, one of bounty, perfection, eternity, and Light. And lastly, discovering this reality by all humankind is the very purpose of Creation.

# Appendices

# GLOSSARY

In all of reality, there is nothing but the Creator and the creature, a Light and a vessel, Upper and lower. Kabbalah texts incorporate many names and appellations intended to highlight different aspects of the relationship between them. Here are the principal attributes we can ascribe each of them:

| Creator | Creature |
|---|---|
| Upper Force, Upper Light, Upper, Light, Creator, God, Godliness, The Creator, The Attribute of Bestowal, The Will to Bestow, The Will to Please, The Upper Nature, The Nature of Altruism, The Spiritual Nature, The Attribute of *Bina*, The Giver, The Leader, The Emanator, Providence, Guidance. | *Kli* (Vessel), Creature, Lower, A Soul, The Attribute of Reception, The Will to Receive, The Lower Nature, The Nature of Egoism, The Corporeal Nature, The Physical Nature, The Attribute of *Malchut*, The Receiver. |

Kabbalists discern various incidents, actions, and manners, both from the perspective of the Upper One, and from the perspective of the lower one, ascribing to each of them a unique name. They do this to assist those who discover the Upper World in finding their way in it. This book is written for those that have yet to attain the Upper World; and for this reason the differences between the various appellations are not emphasized.

Each Kabbalistic term carries many interpretations depending on its context and connection to other elements of reality. Hence, the definitions in the glossary are intended to describe the terms only in the context in which they are presented in this book.

| | |
|---|---|
| Abstract Form | The Form of bestowal without the matter it clothes. |
| *Adam* (referring to man or to mankind in general) | The will to receive that obtains the attribute of bestowal and equalizes with the Creator, the Upper Light. The name *Adam* comes from the Hebrew words *Adame la Elyon* ("I will be like the Most High," Isaiah 14:14). |
| *Adam ha Rishon* | The general soul (or system) that contains all particular souls that descend and clothe people's bodies in this world. |
| Adhesion | The outcome of equalizing the form of the creature with that of the Creator. |
| Altruism | The corrected will to receive with the intention to delight the other and to not receive pleasure for itself; the desire to bestow upon others. |
| Attainment | The ultimate degree of understanding; perceiving every single element in a state. |
| Attribute of the Creator | The Attribute of Bestowal. |
| Attribute of the creature | The Attribute of reception. |
| *Aviut* (Thickness) | The measure of will to receive in the creature. |

| | |
|---|---|
| Barrier | The boundary between this world and the spiritual world. |
| Benevolent (Good that does good) | The Creator's attitude toward the creature. |
| Bestowal upon the Creator | Reception of pleasure from the Creator with the intention of bringing Him contentment. |
| Breaking (Sin of *Adam ha Rishon*) | The forming of the intention to enjoy the Light within the creature itself. |
| Clothing (Clothed) | A process by which one attribute assumes the form of another attribute to perform a certain action through it. |
| Corporeality | The desire to delight oneself. |
| *Tikkun* (Correction) | Changing the will to receive into a will to bestow. |
| Creation of the material world | The arrival of the will to receive at the last and lowest degree in its departure from the Creator, from the Form of bestowal. |
| Creator | The degree that one should reach at the end of all the corrections. The Hebrew word *Boreh* (Creator) comes from the words *Bo Re'eh* (come see). This is the degree that one should come and see, meaning attain on one's own. |

| | |
|---|---|
| Creature | The will to receive that discovers its connection to the Creator. |
| Degrees of Attainment | Phases in the correction of the intention in which the Attribute of Bestowal is felt. |
| Division of the soul of *Adam ha Rishon* | The division of the general soul into particular souls, meaning individual desires. When all the desires in *Adam ha Rishon* had a common intention to bestow upon the Creator they were united as one. When the intention in the desires was reversed into an aim for self-gratification, each desire sensed itself separated from the others, and thus the general soul divided. |
| Egoism | The will to receive, the matter of the whole creation, in which there is no good or bad, and which is consciously used with the intention to please oneself (in order to receive). This intention directly or indirectly harms others. |
| End of Correction | The completion of equalizing the creature's form with the Creator's. |
| Equivalence of Form | Acquiring the Attribute of Bestowal instead of the attribute of reception. |
| Essence | The root and the basis of all forms. |
| Eternity | The integration of the will to receive in the Attribute of Bestowal that brings the will to receive a sensation of unlimited reception of Light. |

| | |
|---|---|
| Evolution of the will to receive | This term relates not to the will to receive itself, but to the intention with which it is used. All the desires, from least to greatest, are present within us. These desires awaken in us to the extent that we attain the aim to bestow upon the Creator. In other words, the evolution is in the *intention*; it is the intention that enables us to use additional desires. |
| Filling (Fulfillment) | The sensation of satisfaction in either the will to receive or the will to bestow. |
| Form Clothed in Matter | The Form of bestowal that the will to receive assumes. |
| Forms (Pattern) | Manner of reception or bestowal. |
| From Above Downward | The creation of the will to receive and the diminishing of the Force of Bestowal in the creature. |
| From Below Upward | The prevailing (overcoming) of the Force of Bestowal in the creature. |
| General Law | The Law of Bestowal. This Law encompasses the whole reality and obligates all its parts to equalize their form with it. |
| God | The overall Force of Bestowal that leads all the souls and brings them to equalize with It. It projects the Attribute of Godliness to the receivers. |

| | |
|---|---|
| Godliness, Upper Light, Upper Force | The Attribute of Bestowal that leads reality, containing all the particular laws in the Upper World as well as in our world. |
| *Ibur, Katnut, Gadlut (Ibur, Yenika, Mochin)* (lit. Conception, Suckling, Adulthood) | The three states that the creature experiences from the spiritual birth to the complete correction. |
| Image of the Creator | The sum of corrected intentions in the will to receive. These intentions are felt in the desires as the image of the Creator. |
| In order to bestow | An act with the intention to bring additional pleasure upon another person or upon the Creator. |
| In order to receive | An act with the intention to bring additional pleasure to oneself. |
| Incarnations | The states the souls experience as they clothe bodies in this world. |
| Incorporation (Incorporated) | Bonding (connecting) of inner attributes. |
| Inner Light | The revelation of the Upper Light in the creature according to its measure of equivalence of Form with the Light. |

| | |
|---|---|
| Inner Vessels, Outer Vessels | The picture of reality is perceived and sensed in the creature's vessels. Inner vessels are vessels sufficiently corrected to evoke the sensation of the inner reality. Outer vessels are partially corrected vessels, evoking the depiction of the outer, remote reality, depending on their measure of correction. The more a *Kli* is corrected, the nearer reality feels when perceiving through it; and the less a *Kli* is corrected, the farther reality feels when perceiving through it. |
| Intention (Aim) | Using the will to receive to benefit oneself or to benefit another. |
| Kabbalist | A creature that attains a measure of equivalence of Form with the Creator. |
| *Kli* (Vessel) | The place to receive the filling. |
| Labor (Effort, Exertion) | The efforts of the will to receive to bring the pleasure closer. |
| Light | The Force of Bestowal that operates and fills all the souls. |
| Light that Reforms, Surrounding Light, Light of Correction | The Force that corrects the egoistic nature and elevates it to the Attribute of Bestowal. |
| Love for the Creator | The creature's desire to delight the Creator by every means at its disposal. |

| | |
|---|---|
| Love of Man | The desire to satisfy all the needs of the other without any consideration of oneself. |
| Lower Nature | The will to receive. |
| *Malchut de Ein Sof* (*Malchut* of the world *Ein Sof*) | The general desire of all reality, created by the Upper Light. |
| *Masach* (lit. Screen) | The intention to bestow upon another that overrides the will to receive in the creature. |
| Material world | The reality sensed through the five physical senses. |
| Matter | The will to receive. |
| Nearing the Creator | Obtaining greater measures of the Attribute of Bestowal. |
| Our world | The reality that is felt in the will to receive. |
| *Parsa* | The boundary between the Upper Guidance and Leadership, and the creatures that it operates. The *Parsa* is situated between the world *Atzilut* and the worlds *Beria, Yetzira, Assiya*. |
| *Partzuf* | A structure made of the ten *Sefirot* of the creature that operate in equivalence of Form with the Upper Light. |

| | |
|---|---|
| Patterns (Forms) | Manners of reception or bestowal. |
| Perfection | The state when the creature is in equivalence of Form with the Creator. |
| Person (in this world) | The will to receive is in a state of concealment from the Creator. Hence, this will to receive has no intention to either receive from Him or to give to Him. |
| Pleasure | The result of fulfilling the will to receive. |
| Point in the Heart | The awakening to know the Upper Force. |
| Process of Creation | The process sensed in the will to receive that evolves in equivalence of Form with the Creator. |
| Purpose of Creation | To do the absolute good to His creations, meaning for the creature to reach the state of the Creator. |
| Recognition of Evil | Perceiving the intention to receive for oneself as being detrimental to the spiritual progress of the creature. |
| Reshimot (Reminiscences, Recollections) | The desires before they are realized through the intention. These are "information cells" containing data about states and forms that one will realize in the future. |

| | |
|---|---|
| Restriction (*Tzimtzum*) | The restriction of the will to receive from receiving pleasure for self-gratification. |
| Revelation of the Creator | The disclosure of the Attribute of Bestowal in the will to receive according to the measure of the *Masach* (Screen) that is placed over the will to receive. |
| Root of the Soul | The place of the soul in the system of *Adam ha Rishon*. |
| Sin of *Adam ha Rishon* (Breaking) | The forming of the aim to enjoy the Light within the creature itself. |
| Sixth sense | The soul, the intention to bestow, the *Masach* (Screen). All these terms refer to a spiritual *Kli* that receives and senses the Upper Force according to its measure of equivalence of Form with it. |
| Soul | The will to bestow. |
| Spiritual Birth | Acquiring the first intention to bestow (*Masach*) over the attributes of the creature. |
| Spiritual evolution | The evolution of the intention to bestow contentment upon the Creator, meaning the evolution of the Attribute of Bestowal. |
| Spiritual *Kli* | The place that receives the filling in order to bestow upon another; a means to bestow upon another. |

| | |
|---|---|
| Spirituality | The Attribute of Bestowal and everything that is felt in it. |
| Ten *Sefirot* | The ten parts of the creature. The first nine parts are the qualities of the Light in it, and the tenth part is the will to receive in it. |
| The Upper System | A state in which the will to receive and the Light in it are in reciprocal bestowal, as determined in the Thought of Creation. |
| The world *Ein Sof* | The state in which the soul has an unlimited ability to bestow upon the Creator. |
| This world | The smallest will to receive. It is without the intention to please the Upper Light or to be pleased by it. |
| Thought of Creation | The reason for Creation, pertaining to the purpose of Creation, meaning the final form of the creature. |
| To do good to His creations | The act of the Creator toward the creature. |
| Upper Force, Upper Light, Godliness | The Attribute of Bestowal that leads reality, containing all the particular laws in the Upper World as well as in our world. |
| Upper Nature | The desire to bestow. |
| Upper World, Spiritual World | The state that appears to one who reaches some measure of equivalence of Form with the Upper Force. |

| | |
|---|---|
| Want | The impression of the will to receive from the filling prior to receiving it. |
| Will to bestow | A) The nature of the Upper Light. B) The will to receive that has been corrected in a person by the intention to use it to bestow upon another person or upon the Creator. |
| Will to delight | The intention to bring pleasure to a stranger, outside of the desire, the will to bestow. |
| Will to enjoy | The desire to receive delight and pleasure. |
| Will to receive | Man's nature—the natural desire to fulfill oneself, created through the Upper Light. |
| Wisdom of Kabbalah | The revelation of the relationship between the Light and the *Kli* at every level of the evolution of the *Kli*, from the beginning of the creation of reality to the end of its correction. |
| Worlds | The states one experiences in the process of equalizing one's attributes with the attribute of the Upper Force, the Attribute of Bestowal. |
| Yearning | Addition to the will to receive. It awakens in the creature as a result of its effort to obtain what it wants. |

# KABBALISTS WRITE ABOUT KABBALAH

## Rabbi Moshe Chaim Lutzato (The Ramchal) (1707-1747)

All of man's engagements are guided by a single, intrinsic premise, and the internality dresses within all people. It is what they referred to as "Nature," whose numeric count is the same as "Elohim" (God). And this is the truth that the Creator concealed from the philosophers.

*~Ramchal, The Book of the War of Moses, Rule 15*

## Rabbi Eliahu—The Vilna Gaon (1138-1204)

Our rabbi, [The Vilna Gaon] engaged extensively in the study of the qualities of nature and the studies of the Earth in order to attain the wisdom of the Torah, to sanctify the name of God among the nations, and to bring the redemption closer. From his youth, he manifested wonders in all seven teachings. He also asked and commanded his disciples to study as much as possible of the seven earthly teachings, and that too was in order to raise the wisdom of Israel according to the wisdom of the Torah in the eyes of the nations, as it is written, "for this is your wisdom and your understanding in the sight of the peoples."

*~Rabbi Hillel Shklover*
*in the name of The Vilna Gaon,*
*The Voice of the Turtle-Dove, p. 115*

Concerning the study of the seven teachings, our rabbi had told us: "The Messianic revelation comes hand in hand with the revelation of the wisdom of the Torah, and appears through the disclosure of the secretes of the Torah and the opening of the seven teachings ...This is what is meant in the Zohar (VaYera, 117) that in the year 1840 the gates of wisdom will open from above and the springs of wisdom from below, with the commencement of the gradual Messianic revelation."

*The Voice of the Turtle-Dove, p. 117*

He would often sigh heavily and say, "Why should the nations say, 'Where is the wisdom of Israel?'" He would often whisper to us what those who perceive our Torah do for the glory of the name of God, as the ancient sages from Israel had done. Many of them glorified the name of God through their extensive knowledge in the research of nature's secrets from the Creator's wonders. Many among the righteous of the nations of the world also extolled the wisdom of the sages of the Torah in Israel—the members of the Sanhedrin, the Tanaaim, the Amoraim, etc. and in later generations our rabbi the Rambam, Baal HaTosafot, and others who did much to sanctify the name of God among the nations through their study in earthly research.

*The Voice of the Turtle-Dove, p. 118*

Studying the seven teachings assists in the attainment of the wisdom of the Torah in its secrets, elevates the wisdom of Israel and the sanctification of God's name in the eyes of the nations, and brings redemption nearer.

*The Voice of the Turtle-Dove, p. 118*

To understand and to attain the wisdom of the Torah contained in the upper light of wisdom, it is also necessary to study the seven teachings concealed in the lower world, the world of nature.

*The Voice of the Turtle-Dove, p. 119*

These are the seven teachings: a) the wisdom of calculus, attribute and measurement; b) the wisdom of creation and assemblage; c) the wisdom of medicine and growth; d) the wisdom of reason, grammar and law; e) the wisdom of playing music and sanctity; f) the wisdom of correction and integration; g) the wisdom of BRW

(Between Rain and Wind), and the mental forces. Our rabbi thoroughly knew all these teachings.

*The Voice of the Turtle-Dove*, p. 120

### Rabbi Abraham Yitzhak HaCohen Kook (1865-1935)

Rationality evolves only because beyond the threshold of its consciousness, the hidden does its scientific and moral work. The prevalent assumption that the hidden obscures the clear science and the accurate critique, is false. It is precisely through the hidden, with the might of its singing and the depth of its reason, that the sound foundation of science is erected, innovative and with accurate and poignant criticism. Combining these two opulences with their great wealth—the hidden and the criticism—builds the sound foundation for the upper Godly light that stands above any word and recognition.

~Rabbi Kook, *Orot (Lights)*, p. 92

The more the immanent secrets of the Torah—whether from the perspective of science, from the perspective of emotion, or from the perspective of imagination—appear, spread, and become qualified for regular and constant study, the higher will one's soul and the soul of the world rise.

~Rabbi Kook, *Orot (Lights)*, p. 90

The events of time, the growth of social relations, and the expansion of sciences greatly refined the human spirit.

~Rabbi Kook, *Orot Emuna (Lights of Faith)*, p. 67

Man's future will indeed come, in which he will evolve to such a sound spiritual state, that not only will every profession not hide another, but every science and every sentiment will reflect the entire scientific sea and the entire emotional depth, as this matter really is in the actual reality.

~Rabbi Kook, *Orot Kodesh A (Holy Lights A)*, p. 22

There is a certain sublime virtue, by which the stronger the apparent knowledge becomes, the greater is the strength of the hidden ken.

~Rabbi Kook, *Orot Kodesh A (Holy Lights A)*, p. 65

One should always fill one's intellectual measure of the natural mind in all its qualities, so the content of "a healthy soul in a healthy body" will be kept in its spiritual measure too.

~Rabbi Kook, *Orot Kodesh A (Holy Lights A)*, p. 66

Just as man should be accustomed to material nature and its forces, study its ways and actions by the same rules that govern the world, of which he is part, and which control within him as they control without, so, and even more so, he should (and must) be accustomed to the rules of the spiritual nature, which govern the whole reality, of which he is part.

~Rabbi Kook, 1985
from the notebooks in the manuscripts,
*Treasures of the Raayah (Rav Kook)*, 4, p. 23

The great value of the power of human desire, its degree in reality, and its cruciality is yet to appear through the secrets of the Torah. And this disclosure will be the crown of all science.

~Rabbi Kook, *Orot Kodesh C (Holy Lights C)*, p. 66

The sciences will deal with bringing all the details from the potential to the actual, which the good and honest inclinations that govern the world aspire for, and they are all the needs of worthy material and spiritual life.

~Rabbi Kook, *Orot Teshuva (Lights of Repentance)*, p. 50

Around the year 1923, Professor Einstein visited in the Land of Israel. A meeting was arranged between him and our rabbi, the Raayah Kook. ...the Rav related to the comprehensiveness of the professor's method and commented that it is a common sight in ancient Jewish treasures that some wondrous revelation that astounds the whole humanity is found in some hidden corner of our ancient literature, and especially the occult, whose lightnings soar to the height of conceptual world, transcending every degree of historic evolution in the world of concepts. So also occurred with the wondrous revelation that takes every thinker's breath away with his new relative method, whose origin is already present in the occult and Kabbalah books, and in the commentaries written about them.

...and that Professor Einstein, through the power of his great mind, bridged that great sea and have found in it a path for the ideas and concepts from which paths elicit to all the sciences. Naturally, the professor listened to the words very attentively and with interest. He commented on the philosophical side of the Rav's comment regarding the understanding of his method, which in the end stands at the technical perception of the construction of the entire world.

~2002, Rabbi Shmuel Shulman's description
of the meeting between Rav Kook and Albert Einstein
*Treasures of the Raayah (Rav Kook)*, 1, p. 87

### Rabbi Yehuda Leib HaLevi Ashlag (Baal HaSulam) (1884-1954)

... they have no scientific solution as to how is it possible for a spiritual object to have any kind of contact with physical atoms and to bring them to any kind of motion. ... We need only the wisdom of Kabbalah in order to move a step forward here, in a scientific manner, for all the teachings of the worlds are included in the wisdom of Kabbalah.

~Baal HaSulam, *The Freedom*

...the reincarnation occurs in all objects of the tangible reality, and each object, in its own way, lives an eternal life. And although our senses tell us that everything is transient, it is only how it seems. But in fact there are only incarnations here, as each item does not rest for a moment but incarnates on the wheel of transformation of the form losing nothing of its essence on its way, as physicists have shown.

~Baal HaSulam, *The Peace*

... you can deduce about the wisdom of truth, which contains all the secular teachings within it, which are its seven little daughters.

~Baal HaSulam
*Introduction to the Book The Tree of Life*, item 4

As one cannot sustain one's body without some knowledge of the corporeal arrangements of nature...just so one's soul has no viability in the next world, except by acquiring some knowledge of the arrangements of the nature of the systems of the spiritual worlds. ...One reincarnates until one is granted the attainment of the wisdom of truth through and through.

~Baal HaSulam
*From My Flesh shall I See God*

Science is generally divided into two parts. One is called "Material Knowledge;" the other is called "Formative Knowledge."

...that part of the science that engages in the quality of the materials of reality in both mere substances—without their form—and in substances and their forms together, is called "Formative Knowledge." This knowledge is founded on empiric basis, meaning on evidence and inferences taken from practical experiences, and these practical experiences are taken as its sound basis for true deductions.

The second part of the science, which engages solely in forms abstracted from substances, without any contact with the substances themselves. ...Hence, any scientific learning of this kind is necessarily based only upon a theoretic basis. This means that it does not take from practical experience, but only from research in theoretic negotiation. All the lofty philosophy belongs to this kind. Therefore, many contemporary scholars have abandoned it, since they are unhappy with any negotiation built on theoretic basis. They think it is uncertain for they only consider the empiric foundation to be certain.

Observe, that the wisdom of Kabbalah too is divided into the two above-mentioned parts: the Material Knowledge and the Formative Knowledge. Yet, there great merit here over secular science. This is because here even the part of the Formative Knowledge is built entirely upon the critique of practical reason, meaning on empiric, practical basis.

~Baal HaSulam
*Matter and Form in the Wisdom of Kabbalah*

The wisdom of truth, meaning the wisdom of the Godly revelation, in His ways unto the creatures, as with secular teachings, should be delivered from generation to generation, and each generation adds another link to its former. Thus the wisdom evolves and at the same time becomes adapted for broader expansion among the masses.

~Baal HaSulam
*The Wisdom of Kabbalah and Its Essence*

As the appearance of animals in this world and conducts of sustenance are a wondrous wisdom, so the appearance of the Godly abundance in the world, both the existence of the degrees and their modes of operation, join to make a wondrous wisdom, far more wondrous than the science of physics. This is because the science of physics is merely knowledge of the conducts in a certain species, found in a particular world and unique to its carrier, and no other teaching is included in it.

This is not so in the wisdom of truth, since it is general ken of the general still, vegetative, animate, and speaking, present in all the worlds in all their events and conducts as they were integrated in the thought of the Creator, meaning in the purposeful carriers. Hence, all the teachings in the world, from the least of them unto the greatest of them, are wondrous contained in it. It equalizes all teachings—those far and different from one another as the east from the west. It equalizes them in an order that is the same for all, meaning until the conducts of every teaching must come by its own ways.

For example, the science of physics is arranged precisely according to the order of the worlds and the Sefirot. Similarly, the science of astronomy is arranged by the same order, and so it is with music and so on. Thus, we find that all the teachings are arranged and follow a single connection and a single ratio—they are all similar to it as the child resembles its progenitor. This is why they are contingent upon one another, meaning the wisdom of truth is contingent upon all the teachings, and all the teachings are contingent upon it. This is also why we do not find a single genuine Kabbalist without comprehensive knowledge in all the worldly teachings, as they acquire it from the wisdom of truth itself, as they are contained in it.

~Baal HaSulam
*The Wisdom of Kabbalah and Its Essence*

# PROMINENT SCHOLARS
# WRITE ABOUT KABBALAH

## Johannes Reuchlin (1455-1522)

Reuchlin, a German humanist, political counselor to the Chancellor, a classics scholar and an expert in the ancient languages and traditions (Latin, Greek, and Hebrew) was affiliated with the heads of the Platonic Academia (della Mirandola and others).

"My teacher Pythagoras, who is the father of philosophy, did nevertheless not receive those teachings from the Greeks, but rather he received them from the Jews. Therefore he must be called Kabbalist, [... ] and he himself was the first to convert the name Kabbala, unknown to the Greeks, in the Greek name philosophy."

"Pythagoras' philosophy emanated from the infinite sea of the Kabbalah."

"This is the Kabbala, which does not let us spend our lives on the ground, but rather raises our intellect to the highest goal of understanding."

~Reuchlin, *De Arte Cabbalistica*

## Giovanni Pico della Mirandola (1463-1494)

An Italian scholar and Platonist philosopher whose *De Hominis Dignitate Oratio (Oration on the Dignity of Man)*, composed in 1486, was a characteristic Renaissance work. It reflected his syncretistic method of taking the best elements from other philosophies and combining them in his own work. Additionally, della Mirandola researched Kabbalah, the Bible, and the Koran after reading them in their original languages.

"This true interpretation of the law (vera illius legis interpretatio), which was revealed to Moses in godly tradition, is called

Kabbalah (dicta Cabala est), which to Hebrews is the same as for us receiving (receptio)."

"In whole [ there are ] two sciences - also with a name they honoured them: the one is called ars combinandi and it is a measure of the progress in sciences [... ]. The other one treats the forces of the higher things, which are over the moon, which is the highest part of magia naturalis. The Hebrews also call both of them Cabala [...]"

~Pico della Mirandola, *Conclusions*

## Paulus Ricius (~ 1470-1541)

Ricius, a physician and a professor of philosophy at Pavia University, Austria, served as personal physician and consultant to Maximilian I, Archduke of Austria, German King and Holy Roman emperor, and to Ferdinand I—King of Bohemia and Hungary.

"The ability to interpret the divine and human secrets by a type of the Mosaic law with allegorical sense is called Kabbalah."

"A literal meaning (of a Scripture) submits to the conditions of time and space. Allegorical and kabbalistic - remains for centuries, unbounded by time and space."

~Paulus Ricius, *Introductoria Theoramata Cabalae*

## Philippus Aureolus Paracelsus (1493-1541)

A German-Swiss physician and alchemist, Paracelsus established the role of chemistry in medicine. He is considered one of the founders of modern science.

"Learn artem cabbalisticam, it explains everything!"

~ Paracelsus, *Das Buch Paragranum*

## Christian Konrad Sprengel (1750–1816)

A German botanist and teacher whose studies of reproduction in plants led him to a general theory of fertilization which is still accepted today.

"Adam, the first man, was very familiar with the Kabbalah. He knew the signatures of all things, and hence gave all animals the most suitable names. Therefore the Hebrew language too contains the best names for all animals, which themselves indicate their nature."

~Kurt Sprengel
*Versuch einer Pragmatischen Geschichte der Arzeikunde*

## Raymundus Lullus (1235-1315)

Lullus, a Spanish writer and philosopher born into a wealthy family in Palma, Mallorca, was well educated, and became the tutor of King James II of Aragon. He wrote in Arabic, Latin and Catalan. He wrote treatises on alchemy and botany, Ars Magna, and Llibre de meravelles.

"The Creation, or language, is an adequate subject of the science of Kabbalah... That is why it is becoming clear that its wisdom governs the rest of the sciences.

Sciences such as theology, philosophy and mathematics receive their principles and roots from her. And therefore these sciences (scientiae) are subordinate to that wisdom (sapientia); and their [ = the sciences ] principles and rules are subordinate to her [ = the Kabbalah ] principles and rules; and therefore their [ = the sciences ]mode of argumentation is insufficient without her [ = the Kabbala ]."

~Raymundus Lullus, *Raymundi Lulli Opera*

## Giordano Bruno (1548-1600)

This Italian philosopher, astronomer, mathematician, and occultist was ahead of his time. His theories anticipated modern science. The most notable of these were his theories of the infinite universe and the multiplicity of worlds, in which he rejected the traditional geocentric (Earth-centered) astronomy and intuitively went beyond the Copernican heliocentric (Sun-centered) theory, which still maintained a finite universe with a sphere of fixed stars. Bruno is, perhaps, chiefly remembered for the tragic death he suffered at the stake. A victim of his own beliefs, he maintained his unorthodox ideas when both the Roman Catholic and the Reformed churches were reaffirming rigid Aristotelian and Scholastic principles.

"This Kabbalah first gives an inexpressible name to the highest principle; from it she lets four principles emanate in an emanation of second degree, from which everyone branches out again to twelve [...] as there are innumerable kinds and subspecies. And in such a way they designate with a special name, depending upon their language, a God, an angel, a reason, a power, which governs over each individual species. In this way it is finally revealed that the whole divinity can be affiliated to one original Source, as well as the whole light, which shines originally and independently, and the images, which break in numerous different mirrors as in just as many individual objects can be led back to a formal and ideal principle, the source of those images."

—Giordano Bruno, *Le Opere Italiane*

## Gottfried Wilhelm Leibnitz (1646-1716)

Leibnitz was a German philosopher, mathematician, and political adviser, important both as a metaphysician and as a logician and distinguished also for his independent invention of the differential and integral calculus. In 1661 he entered the University of Leipzig as a law student; there he encountered the ideas of men who had revolutionized science and philosophy, such as Galileo, Francis Bacon, Thomas Hobbes, and René Descartes. In 1666 he wrote *De Arte Combinatoria (On the Art of Combination)*, in which he formulated a model that is the theoretical ancestor of modern computers.

"Since people did not possess the right key to the secret, the thirst for knowledge here eventually led to vanities and superstition of all kinds, from which ultimately developed a kind of Vulgar Cabbala that lies far away from the true one, as well as diverse fantastic theories under the false name of magic; the books are teeming with those."

~Leibnitz
*Hauptschriften zur Grundlegung der Philosophie*

### Friedrich von Schlegel (1772-1829)

German writer, critic and philosopher, contemporary of Goethe, Schiller and Novalis. A pioneer in comparative Indo-European linguistics and comparative philology, Schlegel deeply influenced the early German Romantic Movement. He is generally held to be the person who first established the term *romantisch* in the literary context.

"The true esthetics is Kabbalah."

~Schlegel, *Kritische F. Schlegel-Ausgabe*
*publisher: Ernst Behler 35 Bde., Paderborn*
(quote from December, 1802)

### Johann Wolfgang von Goethe (1749-1832)

Johann Wolfgang Goethe is widely recognized as the greatest writer of the German tradition. The Romantic period in Germany (the late eighteenth and early nineteenth centuries) is known as the Age of Goethe, and Goethe embodies the concerns of the generation defined by the legacies of Jean-Jacques Rousseau, Immanuel Kant, and the French Revolution. His stature derives not only from his literary achievements as a lyric poet, novelist, and dramatist, but also from his often significant contributions as a scientist (geologist, botanist, anatomist, physicist, historian of science) and as a critic and theorist of literature and art. For the last thirty years of his life he was Germany's greatest cultural icon, serving as an object of pilgrimage from all over Europe and the United States.

"The kabbalistic treatment of the Bible is a hermeneutics, which lives up in a convincing way to the independence, the marvelous originality, the versatility, the totality, I would even say immeasurability of its contents."

~Goethe
*Materialien zur Geschichte der Farbenlehre*

# FURTHER READING

***Basic Concepts in Kabbalah:*** By reading in this book, one develops internal observations and approaches that did not previously exist within. This book is intended for contemplation of spiritual terms. To the extent that we are integrated with these terms, we begin to unveil the spiritual structure that surrounds us, almost as if a mist had been lifted.

***A Guide to the Hidden Wisdom of Kabbalah:*** provides the reader with a solid foundation for understanding the role of Kabbalah in our world. The content was designed to allow individuals all over the world to begin traversing the initial stages of spiritual ascent toward the apprehension of the upper realms.

***Attaining the Worlds Beyond:*** is a first step toward discovering the ultimate fulfillment of spiritual ascent in our lifetime. This book reaches out to all those who are searching for answers, who are seeking a logical and reliable way to understand the world's phenomena. This magnificent introduction to the wisdom of Kabbalah provides a new kind of awareness that enlightens the mind, invigorates the heart, and moves the reader to the depths of their soul.

***Awakening to Kabbalah:*** a distinctive, personal, and awe-filled introduction to an ancient wisdom tradition. Rav Laitman—a disciple of the great Kabbalist Rabbi Baruch Ashlag (son of Yehuda Ashlag)—provides you with a deeper understanding of the fundamental teachings of Kabbalah, and how you can use this wisdom to clarify your relationship with others and the world around you.

Using language both scientific and poetic, he probes the most profound questions of spirituality and existence. This provocative, unique guide will inspire and invigorate you to see beyond the world as it is and the limitations of your everyday life, become closer to the Creator, and reach new depths of the soul.

**The Kabbalah Experience:** Never has the language of Kabbalah been as clear and accessible as it is here, in this compelling, informative collection. The depth of wisdom revealed in the questions and answers of this book will inspire reflection and contemplation. Readers will also begin to experience a growing sense of enlightenment while simply absorbing the words on every page.

*The Kabbalah Experience* is a guide from the past to the future, revealing situations that all students of Kabbalah will experience at some point on their journeys. For those who cherish every moment in life, the author offers unparalleled insights into the timeless wisdom of Kabbalah.

**The Path of Kabbalah:** "Thou shalt not make unto thee a graven image, nor any manner of likeness" (Exodus 20:3). This prohibition from the Bible is also the basis of the Wisdom of Kabbalah. Kabbalists state that there is no reality at all, but something called His Essence, the Upper Force.

As uncanny as it sounds, this notion hides in its wings the very prospect of freedom, for every person, for every nation, and for the entire world. The structure and the perception of reality are the surface of this book.

But the story of humanity, or more accurately, of the human soul, is the undercurrent that drives the reader forward in this book. It is about you; about me; about all of us. This book is about the way we were, the way we are, the way we will be, and most importantly, it is about the best way to get there.

**The Science of Kabbalah:** is the first in a series of texts that Rav Michael Laitman, Kabbalist and scientist, designed to introduce readers to the special language and terminology of the Kabbalah. Here, Rav Laitman reveals authentic Kabbalah in a manner that is both rational and mature. Readers are gradually led to an understanding of the logical design of the Universe and the life whose home it is.

*The Science of Kabbalah,* a revolutionary work that is unmatched in its clarity, depth, and appeal to the intellect, will enable readers to approach the more technical works of Baal Ha-Sulam (Rav Yehuda Ashlag), such as *Talmud Eser Sefirot* and *Zohar.* Although scientists and philosophers will delight in its illumination, laymen will also enjoy the satisfying answers to the riddles of life that only authentic Kabbalah provides. Now, travel through the pages and prepare for an astonishing journey into the Upper Worlds.

**Introduction to the Book of Zohar:** is the second in a series written by Kabbalist and scientist Rav Michael Laitman, which will prepare readers to understand the hidden message of *"The Zohar".* Among the many helpful topics dealt with in this companion text to *The Science of Kabbalah,* readers are introduced to the "language of roots and branches," without which the stories in *The Zohar* are mere fable and legend. Introduction to *The Book of Zohar* will certainly furnish readers with the necessary tools to understand authentic Kabbalah as it was originally meant to be, as a means to attain the Upper Worlds.

**Wondrous Wisdom:** This book presents the first steps, an initial course on Kabbalah, based solely on authentic teachings passed down from Kabbalist teacher to student over thousands of years. Offered within is a sequence of lessons revealing the nature of the wisdom and explaining the method of attaining it. For every person questioning "Who am I really?" and "Why am I on this planet?" this book is an absolute must.

**Kabbalah for Beginners:** By reading this book you will be able to take your first step in understanding the roots of human behaviour and the laws of nature. The contents present the essential principals of the Kabbalistic approach and describe the wisdom of Kabbalah and the way it works. *Kabbalah for Beginners* is intended for those searching for a sensible and reliable method of studying the phenomenon of this world for those seeking to understand the reason for suffering and pleasure, for those seeking answers to the major questions in life. Kabbalah is an accurate method to investigate and define man's position in the universe.

The wisdom of Kabbalah tells us why man exists, why he is born, why he lives, what the purpose of his life is, where he comes from, and where he is going after he completes his life in this world.

# ABOUT BNEI BARUCH

Bnei Baruch is a non-profit organization that is spreading the wisdom of Kabbalah to accelerate the spirituality of humankind. Kabbalist Rav Michael Laitman, PhD, who was the disciple and personal assistant to Rabbi Baruch Ashlag, the son of Rabbi Yehuda Ashlag (author of *The Sulam* commentary on *The Zohar*), follows in the footsteps of his mentor in leading the group toward its mission.

Laitman's scientific method provides individuals of all faiths, religions, and cultures with the precise tools necessary for embarking on a captivating path of self-discovery and spiritual ascent. With the focus being primarily on inner processes that individuals undergo at their own pace, Bnei Baruch welcomes people of all ages and lifestyles to engage in this rewarding process.

In recent years, a massive worldwide search for the answers to life's questions has been underway. Society has lost its ability to see reality for what it is and in its place superficial and often misleading concepts have appeared. Bnei Baruch reaches out to all those who are seeking awareness beyond the standard, people who are seeking to understand our true purpose for being here.

Bnei Baruch offers practical guidance and a reliable method for understanding the world's phenomena. The authentic teaching method, devised by Rabbi Yehuda Ashlag, not only helps overcome the trials and tribulations of everyday life, but initiates a process in which individuals extend themselves beyond their present boundaries and limitations.

Rabbi Yehuda Ashlag left a study method for this generation, which essentially "trains" individuals to behave as if they have already achieved the perfection of the Upper Worlds while still here in our world. In the words of Rabbi Yehuda Ashlag, "This method is a practical way to attain the Upper World, the source of our existence, while still living in this world."

A Kabbalist is a researcher who studies his or her own nature using this proven, time-tested and accurate method. Through this method, one attains perfection and control over one's life, and realizes life's true goal. Just as a person cannot function properly in this world without having knowledge of it, the soul cannot function properly in the Upper World without knowledge of it. The wisdom of Kabbalah provides this knowledge.

## HOW TO CONTACT BNEI BARUCH

Bnei Baruch
1057 Steeles Avenue West, Suite 532
Toronto, ON, M2R 3X1
Canada

E-mail: info@kabbalah.info

Web site: www.kabbalah.info

Toll free in Canada and USA:
1-866-LAITMAN
Fax: 1-905 886 9697